Introduction

Dear Food Enthusiasts,

Welcome to a gateway of culinary discovery and simplicity with the "Ninja Dual Zone Air Fryer Cookbook for Beginners." As the author of this hands-on guide, I am delighted to accompany you as you unlock the full potential of one of the most versatile kitchen gadgets of our time: the Ninja 2-Basket Air Fryer. This book is your starting point for over 189 healthy, delicious recipes designed for the hustle and bustle of modern life.

Embarking on this journey, you hold in your hands not just a cookbook, but a new way of thinking about and preparing food. Whether you're a busy professional, a parent juggling the demands of home, or simply someone looking to step into the world of cooking without feeling overwhelmed, this book is for you.

The Ninja Dual Zone Air Fryer is a marvel of culinary engineering, allowing you to cook two dishes at once, each in their own zone, with different timings and temperatures. It's about to make your cooking quicker, healthier, and more convenient, without compromising on flavor. This book leverages that capability to its fullest, ensuring that every meal is an opportunity to nourish your body, delight your palate, and impress your loved ones.

Designed with beginners in mind, this cookbook demystifies the process of air frying with easy-to-follow, step-by-step guides and tips to make you feel confident in your cooking skills. From mains to sides, from snacks to desserts, and not forgetting vegetarian delights, every recipe is crafted to ensure you make the most out of your Ninja Air Fryer from the get-go.

As we embark on this journey together, remember that cooking is an adventure. It's about exploration, making memories, and the joy of sharing. The "Ninja Dual Zone Air Fryer Cookbook for Beginners" is more than a collection of recipes; it's a companion in your culinary adventure. It's about transforming the mundane into the extraordinary, one meal at a time.

So, let's turn the page and begin this delicious journey together. Here's to creating effortless, healthy, and sumptuous meals that bring joy to your table and love to your home.

Happy Cooking,

NINJA DUAL ZONE AIR FRYER

The Ninja Foodi Dual Zone Air Fryer is a versatile kitchen appliance that allows you to air fry, roast, bake, reheat and more using little to no oil. With its DualZone technology, it provides the functionality of two air fryers in one compact unit, allowing you to cook multiple foods at the same time.

Air frying technology circulates hot air around the food to create a crisp exterior without needing to submerge the food in oil. This makes it a much healthier alternative to deep frying. The twin drawers and separate heating zones of the Ninja Dual Zone Air Fryer take this a step further, enabling you to cook two different foods or larger quantities simultaneously while retaining crispness.

Other standout features include seven built-in Smart Programs for common foods like fries and chicken. These programs automatically set the ideal temperature and time for delicious results with minimal effort. Advanced convenience features also allow you to perfectly synchronize the two zones when cooking different foods together.

In addition to air frying, the Ninja Dual Zone model can serve as a convection oven, allowing you to bake, roast, reheat and more. Programmable controls provide precise temperature regulation between 80°C to 200°C. Additional accessories like the multi-layer rack make it possible to prepare entire meals from appetizers to desserts in one compact countertop appliance.

With quick and easy clean up and space-saving vertical design, the Ninja Dual Zone Air Fryer is a powerful and versatile kitchen assistant. Its oil-free cooking methods result in healthier meals for the whole family that retain their natural juices and crisp texture without needing to deep fry.

FREQUENTLY ASKED QUESTIONS

1. Can the air fryer be used to cook large quantities of food?
- Yes, the Dual Zone model allows you to cook twice as much food at once compared to a single drawer air fryer. You can also use the Sync function to cook large quantities of the same food simultaneously.

2. How do I clean the inside of the air fryer?
- Simply wipe down the inner surfaces of the main unit with a damp cloth or non-abrasive sponge as needed. Be sure to unplug the appliance first. Do not immerse the base in water.

3. Is there a way to check on food without opening the drawer?
- Yes, during cooking you can briefly open the drawer to shake or flip foods for even crisping without pausing the timer. Just be sure to close it quickly within 10 seconds.

4. Which foods are best for air frying?
- Many types of meats, seafood, vegetables and snacks cook beautifully in an air fryer. Popular choices include fries, chicken wings, Brussels sprouts, salmon and cake. Experiment to discover your favorite crispy treats.

5. How do I know when food is fully cooked?
- Use a food thermometer to check internal temperatures according to health code standards. Visual cues like bubbling, browning and crisping can also indicate your air fried foods are ready.

6. Does the non-stick coating require special care?
- No, simply clean the drawers and crisper plates as usual. Avoid abrasive cleaners or scouring pads which could damage the non-stick surfaces over time with excessive scrubbing.

NINJA DUAL ZONE'S DIFFERENT

- Dual cooking zones - It has two independent cooking baskets/drawers instead of one, allowing you to cook double the amount of food simultaneously.

- Sync and Match functions - These features perfectly synchronize the cooking times when using both zones, or match the settings when cooking the same food in both zones. Single drawer models don't have this option.

- Increased versatility - With two cooking zones, you can air fry different foods together or use different functions (air fry, bake, roast etc.) in the separate baskets. This isn't possible with one drawer.

- Larger capacity - The two drawers combined offer more interior space, so you can cook larger portions or an entire meal's worth of side dishes at once.

- Faster meal prep - It dramatically cuts down on cook time by letting you air fry twice as much in the same timeframe compared to using a single drawer consecutively.

- Easier multi-tasking - You don't need to monitor and flip foods as often since both baskets are cooking simultaneously rather than one after the other.

- Compact design - Despite hosting two baskets, it doesn't take up much more countertop space than a regular single basket model.

- More consistent results - The twin zoned heating/frying helps foods cook more evenly in larger quantities than possible with one basket.

This book is published in black and white, without images, with the aim of optimizing the selling price for customers and contributing to environmental protection by minimizing the harmful effects of color ink. While some customers may prefer colorful books, we kindly ask for your understanding in this matter. We hope to receive your interest in more premium publications in the future. We sincerely thank you.

Traditional Dishes

- Bangers and Mash — 1
- Beef Wellington Bites — 1
- Breaded Mushrooms — 2
- Bubble and Squeak — 2
- Chicken and Leek Pie — 3
- Chicken Tikka Masala — 3
- Corned Beef Hash — 4
- Cornish Pasty — 4
- Full English Breakfast — 5
- Potted Shrimp Crostini — 5
- Pork and Apple Hand Pie — 6
- Roast Beef — 6
- Roast Potatoes — 7
- Sausage Rolls — 7
- Scotch Eggs — 8
- Shepherd's Pie — 8
- Steak and Kidney Pie — 9
- Sticky Toffee Pudding — 9
- Toad in the Hole — 10
- Welsh Rarebit — 10

Breakfasts Recipes

- Air Fryer Breakfast Potatoes — 11
- Bacon and Cheese Croissants — 11
- Bacon and Egg Breakfast Tarts — 12
- Bacon-Wrapped Dates — 12
- Banana Pancake Bites — 13
- Black Pudding Slices — 13
- Blueberry Pancakes — 14
- Breakfast Burrito Bowls — 14
- Breakfast Pizza — 15
- Breakfast Quesadillas — 15
- Breakfast Sausage Balls — 16
- Breakfast Sausage Patties — 16
- Cheesy Breakfast Biscuits — 17
- Cheesy Breakfast Potatoes — 17
- Cinnamon French Toast Sticks — 18
- Cinnamon Roll Twists — 18
- Egg and Bacon Breakfast Pies — 19
- Egg and Bacon Muffins — 19
- Egg and Spinach Breakfast Cups — 20
- Egg and Veggie Breakfast Wraps — 20
- Egg Muffins — 21
- Egg-in-a-Hole — 21
- English Muffin Breakfast Sandwiches — 22
- Fruit and Nut Granola — 22
- Hash Browns — 23
- Sausage and Egg Breakfast Burritos — 23

Poultry

- BBQ Chicken Drumsticks — 24
- Buffalo Chicken Wings — 24
- Chicken and Vegetable Skewers — 25
- Chicken Burgers — 25
- Chicken Caesar Pizza — 26
- Chicken Caesar Salad — 26
- Chicken Caesar Wraps — 27
- Chicken Cordon Bleu — 27
- Chicken Drumsticks — 28
- Chicken Enchiladas — 28

- Chicken Fajitas — 29
- Chicken Fritters — 29
- Chicken Goujons — 30
- Chicken Kebabs — 30
- Chicken Kiev — 31
- Chicken Nuggets — 31
- Chicken Parmesan — 32
- Chicken Quesadillas — 32
- Chicken Satay — 33
- Chicken Stir-Fry — 33
- Chicken Stuffed Peppers — 34
- Chicken Tenders — 34
- Chicken Teriyaki — 35
- Chicken Wings — 35
- Honey Mustard Chicken — 36
- Lemon Pepper Chicken Wings — 36
- Lemon Garlic Chicken — 37
- Pesto Chicken Pasta — 37
- Roast Chicken Pieces — 38
- Tandoori Chicken — 38

Fish & Seafood

- Baked Cod with Herbs — 39
- Baked Sea Bass with Lemon and Dill — 39
- Blackened Cajun Tilapia — 40
- Cajun Salmon Fillets — 40
- Coconut Curry Shrimp — 41
- Coconut Crusted Fish — 41
- Cod Fillets — 42
- Fish Burger Patties — 42
- Fish Tandoori Skewers — 43
- Garlic Parmesan Crusted Salmon — 43
- Grilled Halibut Steaks — 44
- Grilled Lobster Tails — 44
- Grilled Mackerel — 45
- Haddock Fillets — 45
- Lemon Garlic Butter Cod — 46
- Mustard-Crusted Salmon — 46
- Plaice Fillets — 47
- Pesto Grilled Swordfish — 47
- Shrimp and Crab Linguine — 48
- Sea Bass Fillets — 48
- Shrimp and Vegetable Stir-Fry — 49
- Shrimp Fried Rice — 49
- Teriyaki Salmon Skewers — 50
- Thai Red Curry Fish — 50
- Trout Fillets — 51
- Tuna Salad Sandwiches — 51

Beef, Pork, and Lamb

- Beef Steak — 52
- Beef Stir-Fry with Vegetables — 52
- Beef and Ale Pie — 53
- Beef and Guinness Pie — 53
- Beef Brisket — 54
- Beef Teriyaki Stir-Fry — 54
- Roast Beef and Yorkshire Pudding — 55
- Beef and Broccoli — 55
- Air-Fried Beef Schnitzel — 56
- Beef Fajitas — 56
- Beef Satay Skewers — 57
- Beef Kebabs — 57
- Pork and Apple Burgers — 58
- Pulled Pork Sliders — 58
- Pork and Mushroom Pie — 59

- Pork Satay Skewers — 59
- Pork Belly Bites — 60
- Pork and Cabbage Dumplings — 60
- Pork and Black Pudding Scotch Eggs — 61
- Pork Stuffed Bell Peppers — 61
- Pork and Vegetable Spring Rolls — 62
- Lamb Souvlaki Skewers — 62
- Lamb Curry — 63
- Lamb and Mint Meatloaf — 63
- Lamb Kofta Kebabs — 64
- Lamb and Potato Hash — 64
- Lamb Chilli Con Carne — 65
- Lamb Shawarma — 65

Appetizers & Snacks

- Arancini Balls — 66
- Avocado Fries — 66
- Bruschetta — 67
- Caprese Skewers — 67
- Cheese Straws — 68
- Chicken Satay Skewers — 68
- Crackers and Cheese — 69
- Crispy Calamari — 69
- Falafel — 70
- Garlic Bread — 70
- Garlic Parmesan Knots — 71
- Halloumi Fries — 71
- Jalapeno Poppers — 72
- Mini Meatballs — 72
- Mini Quiches — 73
- Mozzarella Sticks — 73
- Onion Rings — 74
- Pizza Bites — 74
- Potato Skins — 75
- Samosas — 75
- Spring Rolls — 76
- Stuffed Potato Bites — 76
- Tempura Vegetables — 77
- Yorkshire Puddings — 77

Desserts

- Blueberry Scones — 78
- Bread Pudding — 78
- Cherry Bakewell Tarts — 79
- Chocolate Chip Cookies — 79
- Cinnamon Rolls — 80
- Coconut Macaroons — 80
- Custard Tarts — 81
- Lemon Drizzle Cakes — 81
- Mini Eclairs — 82
- Chelsea Buns — 82
- Mixed Berry Crumbles — 83
- Nutella-Stuffed Doughnuts — 83
- Orange and Almond Cakes — 84
- Peach Cobbler — 84
- Pear and Almond Galettes — 85
- Pineapple Upside-Down Cakes — 85
- Raspberry Hand Pies — 86
- Strawberry Shortcakes — 86
- Apple Crisp — 87
- Jam Roly Poly — 87
- Eton Mess Balls — 88
- Flapjacks — 88
- Bread and Butter Pudding — 89
- Banoffee Pie Bites — 89

Bangers and Mash

Prep: **10** Min | Cook: **15** Min | Serves: **4**

Ingredient:

- 8 pork sausages
- 1 kg potatoes, peeled and chopped into chunks
- 50g unsalted butter
- 100ml milk
- Salt and pepper, to taste
- Gravy, to serve
- Peas or other vegetables, to serve

Instruction:

1. In Zone 1 of the air fryer, place the pork sausages.
2. Select Zone 1, choose the AIR FRY program, and set the temperature to 200°C. Set the time to 15 minutes for cooking the sausages.
3. Press the START/STOP button to begin air frying the sausages.
4. While the sausages are cooking, place the chopped potatoes in a pot of salted water. Bring to a boil and cook until the potatoes are tender.
5. Drain the cooked potatoes and return them to the pot.
6. Add the unsalted butter and milk to the pot with the potatoes.
7. Mash the potatoes, butter, and milk together until smooth and creamy. Season with salt and pepper to taste.
8. Once the sausages are cooked, carefully remove them from Zone 1 of the air fryer.
9. Serve the **bangers and mash** on individual plates, placing the sausages on top of a bed of creamy mashed potatoes.
10. Serve with gravy and peas or other vegetables of your choice.

Chapter 01: Traditional Dishes

Beef Wellington Bites

Prep: **30** Min | Cook: **15** Min | Serves: **12 bites**

Ingredient:

- 300g beef fillet, trimmed and cut into small cubes (about 2cm)
- Salt and pepper, to taste
- 1 tablespoon olive oil
- 1 shallot, finely chopped
- 100g mushrooms, finely chopped
- 1 tablespoon Dijon mustard
- 1 sheet puff pastry, thawed
- 1 egg, beaten (for egg wash)

Instruction:

1. Season the beef fillet cubes with salt and pepper. Heat olive oil in a pan over medium-high heat. Add the beef cubes and sear on all sides until browned. Remove and set aside. Add finely chopped shallot and mushrooms to the pan. Sauté until the mushrooms release their moisture and the mixture is dry. Season with salt and pepper. Remove from heat and let cool slightly.
2. Roll out the puff pastry sheet on a lightly floured surface to a thickness of about 3mm. Cut the puff pastry into small squares, large enough to enclose the beef cubes.
3. Brush each puff pastry square with a thin layer of Dijon mustard.
4. Place a spoonful of the mushroom mixture in the center of each puff pastry square. Place a seared beef cube on top of the mushroom mixture. Fold the corners of the puff pastry squares towards the center, sealing the beef and mushroom filling inside. Press to secure the edges.
5. Evenly dividing beef Wellington bites between the two zone, leaving space between each bite. Select Zone 1, choose the AIR FRY program, and set the temperature to 200°C. Set the time to 15 minutes. Select MATCH to duplicate settings across both zones. Press the START/STOP button to begin cooking.
6. After 15 minutes, carefully remove the **beef Wellington bites** from the air fryer. They should be golden brown and cooked to your desired level of doneness. Allow the bites to cool slightly before serving.

Breaded Mushrooms

Prep: **15** Min | Cook: **15** Min | Serves: **4**

Ingredient:

- 250g button mushrooms
- 100g plain flour
- 2 eggs, beaten
- 150g breadcrumbs
- 1 teaspoon dried mixed herbs
- Salt and pepper, to taste
- Oil or cooking spray, for greasing

Instruction:

1. Clean the button mushrooms and trim the stems.
2. In separate bowls, place the plain flour, beaten eggs, and breadcrumbs mixed with dried mixed herbs.
3. Season the flour with salt and pepper.
4. Grease Zone 1 of the air fryer with oil or cooking spray.
5. Dip each mushroom into the flour, shaking off any excess.
6. Next, dip the flour-coated mushroom into the beaten eggs, ensuring it is fully coated.
7. Finally, roll the mushroom in the breadcrumb mixture, pressing lightly to adhere the breadcrumbs.
8. Place the breaded mushrooms in Zone 1 of the air fryer.
9. Select Zone 1, choose the AIR FRY program, and set the temperature to 200°C. Set the time to 12-15 minutes for cooking the breaded mushrooms.
10. Press the START/STOP button to begin air frying the mushrooms.
11. After 12-15 minutes, carefully open the air fryer and check the breaded mushrooms. They should be golden brown and crispy.
12. If needed, continue cooking for an additional 1-2 minutes until the mushrooms are fully cooked and the breadcrumbs are nicely browned.
13. Remove the **breaded mushrooms** from the air fryer and serve hot with your favorite dipping sauce.

Chapter 01: Traditional Dishes

Bubble and Squeak

Prep: **15** Min | Cook: **20** Min | Serves: **4**

Ingredient:

- 500g potatoes, cooked and mashed
- 250g cooked cabbage, finely chopped
- 1 onion, finely chopped
- 50g butter
- Salt and pepper, to taste
- Oil or cooking spray, for greasing
- Optional: cooked leftover meat (such as roast beef or ham), chopped

Instruction:

1. In a large mixing bowl, combine the mashed potatoes, cooked cabbage, onion, and optional leftover meat (if using). Mix well.
2. Season the mixture with salt and pepper to taste.
3. Grease Zone 1 of the air fryer with oil or cooking spray.
4. Shape the potato and cabbage mixture into small patties, approximately 2-3cm thick.
5. Place the patties in Zone 1 of the air fryer.
6. Select Zone 1, choose the AIR FRY program, and set the temperature to 200°C. Set the time to 15-20 minutes for cooking the bubble and squeak.
7. Press the START/STOP button to begin air frying the bubble and squeak.
8. After 15-20 minutes, carefully open the air fryer and check the bubble and squeak. The patties should be golden brown and crispy on the outside.
9. If needed, continue cooking for an additional 2-3 minutes until the bubble and squeak is fully cooked and heated through.
10. Remove the **bubble and squeak** from the air fryer and serve hot.

Chicken and Leek Pie

Prep: **20** Min | Cook: **30** Min | Serves: **4**

Ingredient:

- 500g boneless, skinless chicken breasts, diced
- 2 leeks, thinly sliced
- 250ml chicken stock
- 150ml double cream
- 25g butter
- 25g plain flour
- Salt and pepper, to taste
- 1 sheet of ready-made puff pastry, thawed if frozen
- 1 egg, beaten (for egg wash)
- Oil or cooking spray, for greasing

Instruction:

1. Grease Zone 1 with oil or cooking spray. In Zone 1, place diced chicken breasts and sliced leeks. Select Zone 1, choose the AIR FRY program, and set the temperature to 200°C. Set the time to 8-10 minutes for cooking the chicken and leeks. Press START/STOP button to begin air frying the chicken and leeks.
2. While the chicken and leeks are cooking, melt butter in a separate saucepan over medium heat. Stir in plain flour to form a roux. Gradually whisk in chicken stock and double cream to create a smooth sauce. Cook, stirring continuously, until thickened. Season with salt and pepper.
3. Remove chicken and leeks from Zone 1 and mix them into the sauce. Grease a pie dish and transfer the chicken and leek mixture into it. Place puff pastry over the pie dish, trimming and crimping edges to seal. Brush beaten egg over pastry for a golden finish.
4. Grease Zone 2 with oil or cooking spray and place the pie dish in Zone 2. Select Zone 2, choose the BAKE program, and set the temperature to 180°C for 15-20 minutes. Press START/STOP.
5. After 15-20 minutes, carefully open the air fryer and check the pastry. It should be puffed up and golden brown.
6. Remove the **chicken and leek pie** from the air fryer and let it cool slightly before serving.

Chapter 01: Traditional Dishes

Chicken Tikka Masala

Prep: **20** Min | Cook: **10** Min | Serves: **4**

Ingredient:

For the chicken marinade:
- 500g boneless, skinless chicken breasts,
- 200g plain yogurt
- 2 tablespoons tikka masala paste

For the tikka masala sauce:
- 2 tablespoons vegetable oil
- 1 onion, finely chopped
- 2 cloves garlic, minced
- 2 tablespoons tikka masala paste
- 400g canned chopped tomatoes
- 200ml coconut milk
- Salt and pepper, to taste

Instruction:

1. In a bowl, combine the plain yogurt, tikka masala paste, and salt. Mix well to form a marinade.
2. Add the chicken pieces to the marinade and toss until they are well coated. Allow the chicken to marinate for at least 15 minutes.
3. In Zone 1 of the air fryer, place the marinated chicken pieces in a single layer. Select Zone 1, choose the AIR FRY program, and set the temperature to 200°C. Set the time to 20 minutes. Press the START/STOP button to begin cooking.
4. While the chicken is cooking, prepare the tikka masala sauce. In a separate pan, heat vegetable oil over medium heat. Add the finely chopped onion and minced garlic. Sauté until the onion becomes translucent.
5. Add the tikka masala paste to the pan and cook for a minute to release its flavors.
6. Pour in the canned chopped tomatoes and coconut milk. Season with salt and pepper to taste. Simmer the sauce for 10 minutes, allowing the flavors to meld together.
7. After 20 minutes of cooking, transfer the cooked chicken pieces to the pan with the tikka masala sauce. Stir well to coat the chicken with the sauce. Serve the **Chicken Tikka Masala** hot over steamed rice or with naan bread.

Corned Beef Hash

Prep: **15** Min | Cook: **20** Min | Serves: **4**

Ingredient:

- 500g potatoes, peeled and diced into small cubes
- 1 onion, finely chopped
- 200g corned beef, diced
- 2 tablespoons vegetable oil
- 1 teaspoon Worcestershire sauce
- Salt and pepper, to taste
- Fresh parsley, chopped (for garnish)

Instruction:

1. In Zone 1 of the air fryer, place the diced potatoes in the basket. Select Zone 1, choose the AIR FRY program, and set the temperature to 200°C. Set the time to 15 minutes.
2. Press the START/STOP button to begin cooking.
3. While the potatoes are cooking, heat the vegetable oil in a pan over medium heat. Add the chopped onion and sauté until it becomes translucent and lightly golden.
4. Add the diced corned beef to the pan and cook for a few minutes until heated through. Stir in the Worcestershire sauce and season with salt and pepper to taste.
5. Once the potatoes are done cooking in the air fryer, transfer them to the pan with the corned beef mixture. Mix well to combine all the ingredients.
6. In Zone 1 of the air fryer, place the potato and corned beef mixture in the basket. Select Zone 1, choose the AIR FRY program, and set the temperature to 200°C. Set the time to 5 minutes.
7. Press the START/STOP button to begin cooking.
8. After 5 minutes, carefully remove the **Corned Beef Hash** from the air fryer. It should be golden brown and crispy.
9. Garnish with fresh chopped parsley.

Chapter 01: Traditional Dishes

Cornish Pasty

Prep: **20** Min | Cook: **25** Min | Serves: **4**

Ingredient:

For the Pastry:
- 350g plain flour
- 175g unsalted butter, cold and cubed
- 1 teaspoon salt
- 6-8 tablespoons cold water

For the Filling:
- 300g beef steak, diced into small cubes
- 1 onion, finely chopped
- 200g potatoes, peeled and diced into small cubes
- 100g swede (rutabaga), peeled and diced into small cubes
- Salt and pepper, to taste
- 1 egg, beaten (for egg wash)

Instruction:

1. In Zone 1, place diced beef, onion, potatoes, and swede in the basket. Select Zone 1, choose the AIR FRY program, and set the temperature to 200°C. Set the time to 15 minutes. Press START/STOP to begin cooking.
2. While the filling is cooking, prepare the pastry. In a large bowl, combine plain flour and salt. Add cold, cubed butter and rub into the flour until it resembles breadcrumbs. Gradually add cold water, mixing until dough comes together. Be careful not to overwork it. Transfer dough onto a lightly floured surface, knead briefly, and wrap in cling film. Refrigerate for 15 minutes.
3. After the filling has cooked for 15 minutes, remove it from the air fryer and let it cool slightly.
4. Divide pastry dough into 4 portions. Roll each into a circle about 20cm in diameter and 4-5mm thick. Spoon a quarter of the filling onto one half of each pastry circle, leaving a border. Season with salt and pepper. Fold the other half over the filling, crimping edges to seal.
5. Evenly divide pasties between the two zones. Select Zone 1, choose the AIR FRY program, and set the temperature to 200°C. Set the time to 25 minutes. Select MATCH. Press START/STOP to begin cooking.
6. After 25 minutes, carefully remove the **Cornish pasties** from the air fryer. They should be golden brown and cooked through. Let them cool slightly before serving.

Full English Breakfast

Prep: **10** Min | Cook: **15** Min | Serves: **4**

Ingredient:

- 200g bacon rashers
- 200g pork sausages
- 200g mushrooms, sliced
- 200g cherry tomatoes
- 4 large eggs
- 4 slices of black pudding
- 4 slices of bread
- Butter, for spreading
- Salt and pepper, to taste

Instruction:

1. In Zone 1, place the bacon rashers and sausages. Select Zone 1, choose the AIR FRY program, and set the temperature to 180°C. Set the time to 10 minutes. Press the START/STOP.
2. In Zone 2, place the sliced mushrooms and cherry tomatoes. Select Zone 2, choose the AIR FRY program, and set the temperature to 180°C. Set the time to 10 minutes. Press the START/STOP button to begin cooking.
3. While the bacon, sausages, mushrooms, and tomatoes are cooking, prepare the black pudding. In a separate pan, cook the black pudding according to the package instructions.
4. Once the bacon, sausages, mushrooms, and tomatoes are done, remove them from the air fryer and set aside. Keep them warm.
5. In Zone 2, crack the eggs into the air fryer basket. Select Zone 2, choose the AIR FRY program, and set the temperature to 180°C. Set the time to 5 minutes. Press the START/STOP.
6. While the eggs are cooking, toast the bread slices and spread them with butter.
7. Once the eggs are cooked to your desired doneness, remove them from the air fryer.
8. Serve the **Full English Breakfast** by arranging the cooked bacon, sausages, mushrooms, cherry tomatoes, black pudding, eggs, and buttered toast on individual plates. Season with salt and pepper to taste.

Chapter 01: Traditional Dishes

Potted Shrimp Crostini

Prep: **15** Min | Cook: **10** Min | Serves: **4**

Ingredient:

- 200g cooked shrimp, peeled and deveined
- 100g unsalted butter
- 1 tablespoon fresh lemon juice
- 1 teaspoon ground mace
- 1 teaspoon ground nutmeg
- Salt and pepper, to taste
- Baguette, sliced into 1cm thick pieces
- Fresh dill, for garnish

Instruction:

1. In Zone 1 of the air fryer, melt the butter. Add the cooked shrimp, lemon juice, ground mace, and ground nutmeg. Season with salt and pepper.
2. In Zone 2 of the air fryer, place the baguette slices.
3. Select Zone 1, choose the AIR FRY program, and set the temperature to 180°C. Set the time to 5 minutes. Select MATCH. Press the START/STOP button to begin cooking.
4. After 5 minutes, carefully remove the shrimp mixture from the air fryer. It should be heated through and infused with the butter and spices.
5. And carefully remove the baguette slices from the air fryer. They should be toasted and crispy.
6. Using a fork or a food processor, roughly mash the shrimp mixture to create a spreadable consistency.
7. Spread the potted shrimp mixture onto the toasted baguette slices.
8. Garnish with fresh dill. Enjoy your delicious **Potted Shrimp Crostini!**

Pork and Apple Hand Pie

Prep: **15** Min | Cook: **15** Min | Serves: **4**

Ingredient:

- 300g pork mince
- 1 small onion, finely chopped
- 1 apple, peeled, cored, and finely chopped
- 1 teaspoon dried sage
- Salt and pepper, to taste
- 1 sheet ready-made puff pastry, thawed
- 1 egg, beaten (for egg wash)
- Fresh parsley, for garnish

Instruction:

1. In Zone 1, cook pork mince and chopped onion until the meat is browned and the onion is softened. Select Zone 1, choose the AIR FRY program, and set the temperature to 180°C. Set the time to 10 minutes. Press START/STOP.
2. Once the pork mince and onion are cooked, add chopped apple, dried sage, salt, and pepper. Mix well and cook for an additional 2-3 minutes to soften the apple. Remove from the air fryer and allow it to cool slightly.
3. On a lightly floured surface, roll out puff pastry sheet to about 3mm thickness. Cut into equal-sized squares or rectangles, depending on the desired size of your hand pies.
4. Place a spoonful of the pork and apple mixture onto one half of each pastry square. Fold the other half over the filling to create a triangle shape. Use a fork to press and seal the edges of the hand pies. Brush the tops with beaten egg wash.
5. In Zone 2 of the air fryer, place the hand pies. Select Zone 2, choose the AIR FRY program, and set the temperature to 180°C. Set the time to 15 minutes. Press START/STOP to begin cooking.
6. After 15 minutes, carefully remove the **hand pies** from the air fryer. They should be golden brown and crispy. Garnish with fresh parsley.

Chapter 01: Traditional Dishes

Roast Beef

Prep: **10** Min | Cook: **60** Min | Serves: **6**

Ingredient:

- 1.5 kg beef joint (such as topside or sirloin)
- 2 tablespoons vegetable oil
- 1 tablespoon Dijon mustard
- 1 teaspoon dried rosemary
- 1 teaspoon dried thyme
- Salt and pepper, to taste

Instruction:

1. In a small bowl, mix together the vegetable oil, Dijon mustard, dried rosemary, dried thyme, salt, and pepper to create a paste.
2. Grease Zone 1 of the air fryer with oil or cooking spray.
3. Place the beef joint in Zone 1 and rub the paste all over the surface of the meat, ensuring it's evenly coated.
4. Select Zone 1, choose the ROAST program, and set the temperature to 200°C. Set the time based on the desired level of doneness:
- For medium-rare: 20 minutes per 500g of beef
- For medium: 25 minutes per 500g of beef
- For well-done: 30 minutes per 500g of beef
5. Press the START/STOP button to begin air frying the roast beef.
6. After the initial cooking time, use a meat thermometer to check the internal temperature of the beef. For medium-rare, the thermometer should read 55-60°C.
7. If the beef hasn't reached the desired temperature, continue cooking in 5-minute increments until the desired level of doneness is achieved.
8. Once cooked to the desired level, carefully remove the roast beef from Zone 1 and let it rest for 10-15 minutes before carving. This allows the juices to redistribute and ensures a tender roast.
9. Carve the **roast beef** into thin slices and serve.

Roast Potatoes

Prep: **10** Min | Cook: **35** Min | Serves: **4**

Ingredient:

- 1 kg potatoes (such as Maris Piper or King Edward)
- 2 tablespoons vegetable oil
- Salt, to taste

Instruction:

1. Peel potatoes and cut them into evenly sized pieces, about 5 cm in diameter. Place in a large saucepan, cover with cold water, and add a pinch of salt. Bring to a boil over high heat and cook for 5 minutes to partially cook them.
2. Drain potatoes and return them to the saucepan. Shake vigorously to roughen up the edges, creating a crispy exterior. Drizzle with vegetable oil and toss to coat evenly.
3. Grease both zone of the air fryer with oil or cooking spray. Evenly dividing potatoes between the two zone, ensuring they are spread out in a single layer. Select Zone 1, choose the ROAST program, and set the temperature to 200°C. Set the time to 30-35 minutes for roasting the potatoes. Select MATCH. Press the START/STOP button to begin cooking..
4. After 15 minutes of cooking, carefully open the air fryer and shake the potatoes to ensure they cook evenly.
5. Close the air fryer and continue roasting for the remaining time or until the potatoes are golden brown and crispy.
6. Remove the roast potatoes from both zone and transfer them to a serving dish. Sprinkle with salt to taste and toss to evenly distribute the seasoning. Serve the **roast potatoes** hot as a delicious side dish to your meal.

Chapter 01: Traditional Dishes

Sausage Rolls

Prep: **20** Min | Cook: **20** Min | Serves: **6-8**

Ingredient:

- 500g puff pastry
- 500g sausage meat (or sausages with casings removed)
- 1 small onion, finely chopped
- 1 teaspoon dried sage
- Salt and pepper, to taste
- 1 egg, beaten (for egg wash)

Instruction:

1. In a mixing bowl, combine the sausage meat, finely chopped onion, dried sage, salt, and pepper. Mix well until all the ingredients are evenly incorporated.
2. On a lightly floured surface, roll out the puff pastry to a rectangle approximately 30 cm x 40 cm.
3. Cut the pastry into smaller rectangles, about 10 cm x 15 cm each.
4. Place a portion of the sausage mixture along the length of each pastry rectangle, leaving a small border along the edges.
5. Brush the beaten egg along one edge of the pastry.
6. Roll the pastry over the sausage mixture, sealing the edge with the egg-washed side. Press lightly to secure the seal.
7. Grease both zone of the air fryer with oil or cooking spray.
8. Evenly dividing sausage rolls between the two zones, ensuring they are spaced apart.
9. Select Zone 1, choose the BAKE program, and set the temperature to 180°C. Set the time to 15-20 minutes for baking the sausage rolls. Select MATCH. Press the START/STOP button to begin baking the sausage rolls.
10. After about 10 minutes of baking, carefully open the air fryer and brush the sausage rolls with the remaining beaten egg for a shiny finish.
11. Remove the **sausage rolls** and let them cool slightly before serving. Serve the sausage rolls warm as a delightful snack or appetizer.

Scotch Eggs

Prep: **20** Min | Cook: **20** Min | Serves: **6**

Ingredient:

- 6 large eggs
- 500g sausage meat (or sausages with casings removed)
- 50g breadcrumbs
- 50g plain flour
- Salt and pepper, to taste
- Vegetable oil, for greasing
- Optional: 1 teaspoon dried herbs (such as thyme or sage)

Instruction:

1. Place eggs in a saucepan and cover with cold water. Bring to a boil over high heat and cook for 7 minutes for a slightly soft center or 8 minutes for a firmer center.
2. Transfer cooked eggs to a bowl of ice water to cool, making them easier to handle and peel. Peel the cooled eggs..
3. In a mixing bowl, combine sausage meat, breadcrumbs, salt, pepper, and optional dried herbs. Mix well until evenly incorporated. Divide mixture into 6 equal portions.
4. On a lightly floured surface, flatten each portion of sausage meat into a thin patty. Place an egg in the center of each patty and wrap the sausage meat around it, ensuring it is fully covered.
5. Grease Zone 1 of the air fryer with vegetable oil or cooking spray.
6. Place the Scotch eggs in Zone 1, ensuring they are spaced apart.
7. Select Zone 1, choose the AIR FRY program, and set the temperature to 180°C. Set the time to 15-20 minutes for cooking the Scotch eggs. Press the START/STOP.
8. After about 8-10 minutes of cooking, carefully open the air fryer and flip the Scotch eggs to ensure even browning.
9. Serve the **Scotch eggs** warm or at room temperature as a tasty snack or appetizer.

Chapter 01: Traditional Dishes

Shepherd's Pie

Prep: **20** Min | Cook: **30** Min | Serves: **4**

Ingredient:

For the filling:
- 500g lamb mince
- 1 onion, finely chopped
- 2 carrots, peeled and diced
- 2 cloves of garlic, minced
- 1 tablespoon tomato paste
- 200ml beef or vegetable broth
- 1 tablespoon Worcestershire sauce
- 1 tablespoon fresh rosemary, chopped
- Salt and pepper, to taste

For the mashed potato topping:
- 700g potatoes, peeled and cut into chunks
- 50g unsalted butter
- 100ml milk
- Salt and pepper, to taste

Instruction:

1. In Zone 1, cook the lamb mince, onion, carrots, and garlic until the lamb is browned and the vegetables are softened. Select Zone 1, choose the AIR FRY program, and set the temperature to 180°C. Set the time to 10 minutes. Press the START/STOP.
2. Once the lamb is cooked, add the tomato paste, beef or vegetable broth, Worcestershire sauce, fresh rosemary, salt, and pepper. Mix well and cook for an additional 5 minutes to allow the flavors to meld.
3. In the meantime, in Zone 2, place the potato chunks. Select Zone 2, choose the AIR FRY program, and set the temperature to 180°C. Set the time to 15 minutes. Press the START/STOP.
4. After 15 minutes, carefully remove the potato chunks from the air fryer. They should be fork-tender.
5. In a separate bowl, mash the cooked potato chunks with the unsalted butter and milk until smooth and creamy. Season with salt and pepper to taste.
6. Transfer the lamb filling to an oven-safe dish. Spread the mashed potato topping evenly over the filling.
7. Place the dish in Zone 1 of the air fryer. Select Zone 1, choose the AIR FRY program, and set the temperature to 180°C. Set the time to 15 minutes. Press the START/STOP button to begin cooking.
8. After 15 minutes, carefully remove the **Shepherd's Pie** from the air fryer. The mashed potato topping should be golden and crispy.

Steak and Kidney Pie

Prep: **20** Min | Cook: **40** Min | Serves: **4**

Ingredient:

- 500g beef steak, diced into small pieces
- 250g beef kidney, diced into small pieces
- 1 large onion, finely chopped
- 2 cloves of garlic, minced
- 2 carrots, finely chopped
- 200g mushrooms, sliced
- 2 tablespoons flour
- 400ml beef stock
- 2 tablespoons Worcestershire sauce
- 1 teaspoon dried thyme
- Salt and pepper, to taste
- 500g puff pastry
- 1 egg, beaten (for egg wash)

Instruction:

1. In a large pan, heat oil over medium heat. Add chopped onion, garlic, carrots, and mushrooms. Cook until softened, stirring occasionally. Add diced beef steak and kidney. Cook until browned on all sides. Sprinkle flour over meat and vegetables, stirring well to coat. Gradually add beef stock, Worcestershire sauce, dried thyme, salt, and pepper. Stir well and simmer for about 15 minutes to thicken sauce and meld flavors.
2. Grease Zone 1. Transfer steak and kidney mixture to Zone 1, ensuring even spread. Select Zone 1, choose the ROAST program, and set temperature to 180°C for 15-20 minutes. Press START/STOP to begin roasting.
3. While filling is cooking, roll out puff pastry on a lightly floured surface to fit pie dish size. Grease Zone 2 of air fryer. Line pie dish with rolled-out puff pastry, ensuring edges hang over sides.
4. Once filling is cooked, carefully remove from Zone 1 and transfer to pie dish. Fold overhanging edges of puff pastry over filling to encase completely. Brush beaten egg over top for golden finish.
5. Place pie dish in Zone 2. Select Zone 2 and choose the BAKE program, and set temperature to 180°C for 20-25 minutes. Press START/STOP.
6. Serve the **steak and kidney pie** hot as a classic British dish, accompanied by your favorite sides.

Chapter 01: Traditional Dishes

Sticky Toffee Pudding

Prep: **20** Min | Cook: **20** Min | Serves: **6**

Ingredient:

For the pudding:
- 200g dates, pitted and chopped
- 175ml boiling water
- 1 teaspoon bicarbonate of soda
- 75g unsalted butter, softened
- 175g light brown sugar
- 2 large eggs
- 175g self-raising flour
- 1 teaspoon vanilla extract

For the toffee sauce:
- 200g light brown sugar
- 200ml double cream
- 50g unsalted butter

Instruction:

1. In a bowl, combine the chopped dates, boiling water, and bicarbonate of soda. Let it sit for about 10 minutes to soften the dates.
2. In a separate large mixing bowl, cream together the softened butter and light brown sugar until light and fluffy. Add the eggs one at a time, beating well after each addition. Gradually add the self-raising flour to the butter mixture, mixing until just combined. Stir in the softened dates and vanilla extract, ensuring they are evenly distributed throughout the batter.
3. Grease Zone 1 of the air fryer with butter or cooking spray.
4. Transfer the pudding batter to Zone 1, ensuring it is spread out evenly. Select Zone 1, choose the ROAST program, and set the temperature to 180°C. Set the time to 20-25 minutes for baking the sticky toffee pudding. Press the START/STOP.
5. While the pudding is cooking, prepare the toffee sauce. In a saucepan, combine the light brown sugar, double cream, and unsalted butter. Heat over medium heat, stirring constantly, until the sugar has dissolved and the sauce has thickened slightly. Remove from the heat and set aside.
6. Cut the warm pudding into individual portions and serve with the warm toffee sauce poured over the top.
7. Optionally, you can serve the **sticky toffee pudding** with a scoop of vanilla ice cream or a dollop of whipped cream for added indulgence.

Toad in the Hole

Prep: **10** Min | Cook: **30** Min | Serves: **4**

Ingredient:

- 225g plain flour
- 4 large eggs
- 300ml milk
- 8 pork sausages
- 2 tablespoons vegetable oil
- Salt and pepper, to taste
- Optional: Onion gravy, to serve

Instruction:

1. In a large mixing bowl, combine the plain flour, eggs, and milk. Whisk until you have a smooth batter. Season with salt and pepper to taste.
2. In a separate pan, heat the vegetable oil and cook the pork sausages until browned on all sides. Remove from heat and set aside.
3. Grease Zone 1 with oil or cooking spray. Place the cooked sausages in Zone 1, ensuring they are evenly spaced out. Select Zone 1, choose the ROAST program, and set the temperature to 200°C. Set the time to 10 minutes for pre-cooking the sausages. Press the START/STOP.
4. After 10 minutes of pre-cooking, carefully remove the sausages from Zone 1 and pour the batter over them, ensuring the sausages are evenly distributed.
5. Grease Zone 1 with oil or cooking spray. Place the sausage and batter mixture in Zone 1, ensuring it is spread out evenly. Choose the BAKE program, and set the temperature to 200°C. Set the time to 15-20 minutes for baking the Toad in the Hole.
6. While the Toad in the Hole is baking, prepare the optional onion gravy according to your preferred recipe.
7. After 15-20 minutes of baking, carefully open the air fryer and check if the Toad in the Hole is risen and golden brown.
8. Serve the **Toad in the Hole** hot, accompanied by the optional onion gravy.

Chapter 01: Traditional Dishes

Welsh Rarebit

Prep: **10** Min | Cook: **12** Min | Serves: **4**

Ingredient:

- 300g grated cheddar cheese
- 2 tablespoons butter
- 2 tablespoons all-purpose flour
- 1 teaspoon Dijon mustard
- 1 teaspoon Worcestershire sauce
- 4-6 slices of bread
- Optional: Tomato slices and/or cooked bacon, to serve

Instruction:

1. In a saucepan, melt the butter over medium heat. Add the flour and stir continuously for about 1 minute to create a roux.
2. Gradually add the grated cheddar cheese to the roux, stirring well after each addition until the cheese has melted and the mixture is smooth.
3. Stir in the Dijon mustard and Worcestershire sauce, ensuring they are well incorporated into the cheese mixture.
4. Grease Zone 1 of the air fryer with butter or cooking spray.
5. Place the slices of bread in Zone 1. Select Zone 1, choose the ROAST program, and set the temperature to 180°C. Set the time to 3-4 minutes. Press the START/STOP.
6. After 3-4 minutes of pre-toasting, carefully remove the bread from Zone 1 and flip them over.
7. Spread the cheese mixture evenly over the top side of each slice of bread.
8. Place the cheese-topped bread slices in Zone 1. Choose the BAKE function, and set the temperature to 180°C. Set the time to 6-8 minutes.
9. While the Welsh Rarebit is baking, optionally prepare tomato slices and/or cooked bacon to serve as toppings.
10. After 6-8 minutes of baking, carefully open the air fryer and check if the cheese is melted and bubbly.
11. Serve the **Welsh Rarebit** hot, optionally topped with tomato slices and/or cooked bacon.

Air Fryer Breakfast Potatoes

Prep: **10** Min | Cook: **25** Min | Serves: **4**

Ingredient:

- 800g potatoes, peeled and cubed
- 2 tablespoons vegetable oil
- 1 teaspoon paprika
- 1 teaspoon garlic powder
- 1 teaspoon dried thyme
- Salt and pepper, to taste
- Fresh parsley, chopped (for garnish)

Instruction:

1. In a large bowl, combine the cubed potatoes, vegetable oil, paprika, garlic powder, dried thyme, salt, and pepper. Toss until the potatoes are well coated with the seasoning.
2. In Zone 1 of the air fryer, place the seasoned potatoes. Select Zone 1, choose the AIR FRY program, and set the temperature to 200°C. Set the time to 25 minutes.
3. Press the START/STOP button to begin cooking.
4. After 15 minutes of cooking, carefully remove the basket from Zone 1 and give it a shake to ensure even cooking. Return the basket to Zone 1 and continue cooking for the remaining 10 minutes.
5. While the potatoes are cooking, prepare the rest of your breakfast ingredients.
6. After the cooking time is complete, carefully remove the air fryer basket from Zone 1. The potatoes should be crispy and golden brown.
7. Transfer the **breakfast potatoes** to a serving dish, garnish with fresh parsley, and serve hot.

Chapter 02: Breakfasts Recipes

Bacon and Cheese Croissants

Prep: **10** Min | Cook: **15** Min | Serves: **4**

Ingredient:

- 4 croissants
- 8 slices of bacon
- 100g cheddar cheese, grated
- 2 tablespoons butter, melted

Instruction:

1. In Zone 1 of the air fryer, cook the bacon slices until crispy. Select Zone 1, choose the AIR FRY program, and set the temperature to 180°C. Set the time to 10 minutes.
2. Press the START/STOP button to begin cooking.
3. While the bacon is cooking, slice the croissants in half lengthwise.
4. Once the bacon is cooked, remove it from the air fryer and set it aside.
5. In each croissant half, place 2 slices of cooked bacon and sprinkle with grated cheddar cheese.
6. In Zone 2 of the air fryer, place the prepared croissant halves. Select Zone 2, choose the AIR FRY program, and set the temperature to 180°C. Set the time to 5 minutes.
7. Press the START/STOP button to begin cooking.
8. After 5 minutes, carefully remove the croissants from the air fryer. The cheese should be melted and the croissants should be golden.
9. Brush the melted butter over the tops of the croissants for added flavor and shine.
10. Serve the **Bacon and Cheese Croissants** warm and enjoy!

Bacon and Egg Breakfast Tarts

Prep: **15** Min | Cook: **15** Min | Serves: **4**

Ingredient:

- 1 sheet ready-made puff pastry, thawed
- 4 slices of bacon
- 4 large eggs
- 50g cheddar cheese, grated
- Salt and pepper, to taste
- Fresh chives, chopped (for garnish)

Instruction:

1. In Zone 1, cook the bacon slices until crispy. Select Zone 1, choose the AIR FRY program, and set the temperature to 200°C. Set the time to 8 minutes. Press the START/STOP.
2. While the bacon is cooking, roll out the puff pastry sheet on a lightly floured surface. Cut the pastry into 4 equal squares.
3. Place each pastry square into Zone 2 of the air fryer. Select Zone 2, choose the AIR FRY program, and set the temperature to 200°C. Set the time to 5 minutes. Press the START/STOP.
4. Once the bacon is cooked, remove it from the air fryer and set it aside. Crumble or chop the bacon into small pieces.
5. After 5 minutes, carefully remove pastry squares from the air fryer. They should be puffed and golden. Create a well in the center of each pastry square by gently pressing down the center with the back of a spoon. Crack an egg into each pastry square, making sure the egg stays within the well. Sprinkle the crumbled bacon and grated cheddar cheese around the egg. Season with salt and pepper.
6. Return the filled pastry squares to Zone 2. Select Zone 2 and choose the AIR FRY program, and set the temperature to 200°C for 7 minutes. After 7 minutes, carefully remove the **Bacon and Egg Breakfast Tarts** from the air fryer. Garnish with fresh chives and serve the tarts warm.

Chapter 02: Breakfasts Recipes

Bacon-Wrapped Dates

Prep: **15** Min | Cook: **10** Min | Serves: **6**

Ingredient:

- 12 Medjool dates, pitted
- 6 slices of streaky bacon, cut in half lengthwise
- 50g goat cheese
- 12 small pecan halves
- Freshly ground black pepper, to taste

Instruction:

1. Stuff each pitted date with a small amount (about 1 teaspoon) of goat cheese. Place a pecan half on top of the goat cheese.
2. Wrap each stuffed date with a piece of bacon, securing it with a toothpick. Repeat for the remaining dates.
3. In Zone 1 of the air fryer, place the bacon-wrapped dates. Select Zone 1, choose the AIR FRY program, and set the temperature to 200°C. Set the time to 10 minutes.
4. Press the START/STOP button to begin cooking.
5. After 5 minutes of cooking, carefully remove the basket from Zone 1 and give it a shake to ensure even cooking. Return the basket to Zone 1 and continue cooking for the remaining 5 minutes.
6. After the cooking time is complete, carefully remove the air fryer basket from Zone 1. The bacon should be crispy and the dates should be soft and caramelized.
7. Sprinkle freshly ground black pepper over the **bacon-wrapped dates** for added flavor.
8. Allow the dates to cool slightly before serving. Remove the toothpicks before enjoying.

Banana Pancake Bites

Prep: **10** Min | Cook: **8** Min | Serves: **4**

Ingredient:

- 150g self-raising flour
- 1 tablespoon sugar
- 1 ripe banana, mashed
- 150ml milk
- 1 large egg
- Vegetable oil, for greasing
- Maple syrup, for serving

Instruction:

1. In a mixing bowl, combine the self-raising flour and sugar. Add the mashed banana, milk, and egg. Stir well until the batter is smooth and all the ingredients are incorporated.
2. Grease the air fryer baskets with vegetable oil to prevent sticking.
3. Spoon the pancake batter into the air fryer baskets, filling each basket about halfway full. Be sure to keep some space between each pancake bite to allow for even cooking.
4. Select Zone 1, choose the BAKE program, and set the temperature to 180°C. Set the time to 8 minutes. Press the START/STOP button to begin baking the pancake bites.
5. After 4 minutes of baking, open the air fryer and flip the pancake bites using tongs or a spatula to ensure they cook evenly on both sides.
6. Close the air fryer and continue baking for the remaining 4 minutes or until the pancake bites are golden brown and cooked through.
7. Once cooked, carefully remove the pancake bites from the air fryer and let them cool for a minute or two.
8. Serve the **Banana Pancake Bite**s warm with a drizzle of maple syrup.

Chapter 02: Breakfasts Recipes

Black Pudding Slices

Prep: **5** Min | Cook: **10** Min | Serves: **4**

Ingredient:

- 200g black pudding, sliced into rounds (about 1 cm thick)
- Oil, for greasing

Instruction:

1. Lightly grease the air fryer basket with oil to prevent sticking.
2. Place the black pudding slices in Zone 1 of the air fryer basket, making sure they are not overlapping.
3. Select Zone 1, choose the AIR FRY program, and set the temperature to 200°C. Set the time to 10 minutes.
4. Press the START/STOP button to begin cooking.
5. After 5 minutes of cooking, carefully remove the basket from Zone 1 and flip the black pudding slices using tongs. Return the basket to Zone 1 and continue cooking for the remaining 5 minutes.
6. After the cooking time is complete, carefully remove the air fryer basket from Zone 1. The black pudding slices should be crispy and cooked through.
7. Allow the **black pudding slices** to cool slightly before serving.

Blueberry Pancakes

Prep: **10** Min | Cook: **8** Min | Serves: **4**

Ingredient:

- 200g self-raising flour
- 1 tablespoon sugar
- 1 teaspoon baking powder
- 1 large egg
- 200ml milk
- 50g melted butter
- 100g blueberries
- Vegetable oil, for greasing
- Maple syrup, for serving

Instruction:

1. In a mixing bowl, combine the self-raising flour, sugar, and baking powder. In a separate bowl, whisk together the egg, milk, and melted butter.
2. Pour the wet ingredients into the dry ingredients and mix until just combined. Be careful not to overmix; a few lumps are okay. Gently fold in the blueberries.
3. Grease the air fryer baskets with vegetable oil to prevent sticking.
4. Spoon the pancake batter into the air fryer baskets, filling each basket about halfway full. Be sure to keep some space between each pancake to allow for even cooking.
5. Select Zone 1, choose the BAKE program, and set the temperature to 180°C. Set the time to 8 minutes. Press the START/STOP button to begin baking the pancakes.
6. After 4 minutes of baking, open the air fryer and flip the pancakes using tongs or a spatula to ensure they cook evenly on both sides.
7. Close the air fryer and continue baking for the remaining 4 minutes or until the pancakes are golden brown and cooked through.
8. Once cooked, carefully remove the pancakes from the air fryer and stack them on a plate. Serve with a drizzle of maple syrup.
9. Enjoy your **Blueberry Pancakes**!

Chapter 02: Breakfasts Recipes

Breakfast Burrito Bowls

Prep: **15** Min | Cook: **15** Min | Serves: **4**

Ingredient:

For the Burrito Bowls:
- 400g cooked white rice
- 4 large eggs
- 200g canned black beans, rinsed and drained
- 200g cherry tomatoes, halved
- 100g shredded cheddar cheese
- 1 avocado, sliced
- Fresh cilantro, chopped (for garnish)
- Salt and pepper, to taste

For the Salsa:
- 1 small red onion, finely chopped
- 1 jalapeno pepper, seeded and finely chopped
- 2 tablespoons lime juice
- 2 tablespoons fresh cilantro, chopped
- Salt and pepper, to taste

Instruction:

1. In Zone 1 of the air fryer basket, spread the cooked white rice evenly.
2. In Zone 2 of the air fryer basket, crack the eggs and season them with salt and pepper.
3. Select Zone 1, choose the AIR FRY program, and set the temperature to 180°C. Set the time to 10 minutes. Select MATCH. Press the START/STOP button to begin cooking.
4. After 5 minutes of cooking, carefully remove the basket from Zone 1 and give the rice a stir to prevent sticking. Return the basket to Zone 1 and continue cooking for the remaining 5 minutes.
5. In the meantime, prepare the salsa by combining the finely chopped red onion, jalapeno pepper, lime juice, fresh cilantro, salt, and pepper in a bowl. Mix well and set aside.
6. After the cooking time is complete, carefully remove the air fryer basket from Zone 1. The rice should be heated through and slightly crispy, and the eggs should be cooked to your desired doneness.
7. Top each bowl with black beans, cherry tomatoes, shredded cheddar cheese, sliced avocado, and the cooked eggs.
8. Garnish with fresh cilantro and serve with the prepared salsa on the side. Enjoy your flavorful **Breakfast Burrito Bowls**!

Breakfast Pizza

Prep: **10** Min | Cook: **12** Min | Serves: **2**

Ingredient:

- 1 ready-made pizza base (approximately 25cm in diameter)
- 4 slices of bacon, cooked and crumbled
- 4 large eggs
- 100g grated cheddar cheese
- 100g cherry tomatoes, halved
- Fresh basil leaves, chopped (for garnish)
- Salt and pepper, to taste

Instruction:

1. Place the pizza base in Zone 1 of the air fryer basket.
2. In Zone 2, crack the eggs. Season them with salt and pepper.
3. Select Zone 1, choose the AIR FRY program, and set the temperature to 180°C. Set the time to 8 minutes. Select MATCH. Press the START/STOP button to begin cooking.
4. After 4 minutes of cooking, carefully remove the basket from Zone 1 and sprinkle the crumbled bacon evenly over the pizza base. Return the basket to Zone 1 and continue cooking for the remaining 4 minutes.
5. In the meantime, in Zone 2, cook the eggs to your desired doneness. If you prefer soft-cooked eggs, cook them for about 4-5 minutes. For firmer eggs, cook them for 6-7 minutes.
6. After the cooking time is complete, carefully remove the air fryer basket from Zone 1. The pizza base should be crispy and golden.
7. Carefully transfer the cooked eggs onto the pizza base.
8. Top the pizza with grated cheddar cheese and cherry tomato halves.
9. Place back into Zone 1. Choose the AIR FRY program, and set the temperature to 180°C. Set the time to 4 minutes. The cheese should be melted and bubbly, and the tomatoes slightly softened.
10. Garnish with fresh basil leaves and season with additional salt and pepper, if desired. Enjoy your delicious **Breakfast Pizza**!

Chapter 02: Breakfasts Recipes

Breakfast Quesadillas

Prep: **10** Min | Cook: **12** Min | Serves: **2**

Ingredient:

- 4 medium flour tortillas (approximately 20cm in diameter)
- 4 slices of cooked ham, chopped
- 4 large eggs
- 100g grated cheddar cheese
- 1/2 red bell pepper, diced
- 2 spring onions, finely sliced
- Salt and pepper, to taste
- Fresh cilantro, chopped (for garnish)
- Salsa or hot sauce, for serving (optional)

Instruction:

1. In Zone 1 of the air fryer basket, place two flour tortillas.
2. In Zone 2, crack the eggs. Season them with salt and pepper.
3. Select Zone 1, choose the AIR FRY program, and set the temperature to 180°C. Set the time to 6 minutes. Select MATCH. Press the START/STOP button to begin cooking.
4. After 3 minutes of cooking, flip the tortillas. Return the basket to Zone 1 and continue cooking for the remaining 3 minutes.
5. In the meantime, in Zone 2, cook the eggs to your desired doneness. If you prefer soft-cooked eggs, cook them for about 4-5 minutes. For firmer eggs, cook them for 6-7 minutes.
6. After the cooking time is complete, carefully remove the air fryer basket from Zone 1. The tortillas should be slightly crispy.
7. Transfer the cooked eggs onto one of the tortillas.
8. Top the eggs with chopped ham, grated cheddar cheese, diced red bell pepper, and sliced spring onions.
9. Place the remaining two tortillas on top to form quesadilla sandwiches.
10. Place back into Zone 1. Select Zone 1, choose the AIR FRY program, and set the temperature to 180°C. Set the time to 6 minutes. Press the START/STOP button to begin cooking.
11. After the cooking time is complete, the quesadillas should be golden brown and the cheese melted. Cut the quesadillas into wedges and garnish with fresh cilantro. Serve with salsa or hot sauce, if desired. Enjoy your tasty **Breakfast Quesadillas**!

Breakfast Sausage Balls

Prep: **15** Min | Cook: **12** Min | Serves: **20 balls**

Ingredient:

- 300g pork sausage meat
- 100g breadcrumbs
- 1 small onion, finely chopped
- 1 small apple, grated
- 1 tablespoon fresh parsley, chopped
- 1 teaspoon dried sage
- 1/2 teaspoon salt
- 1/4 teaspoon black pepper
- Cooking spray or oil, for greasing

Instruction:

1. In a large bowl, combine the pork sausage meat, breadcrumbs, finely chopped onion, grated apple, fresh parsley, dried sage, salt, and black pepper. Mix well until all the ingredients are evenly distributed.
2. Shape the mixture into small balls, approximately 3cm in diameter.
3. Grease Zone 1 and Zone 2 of the air fryer basket with cooking spray or oil.
4. Place the sausage balls in both zones of the air fryer basket, leaving space between each one.
5. Select Zone 1 and the AIR FRY program. Set the temperature to 180°C and the time to 12 minutes. Select MATCH. Press the START/STOP button to begin cooking.
6. After 6 minutes of cooking, open the air fryer and carefully flip the sausage balls to ensure even browning. Close the air fryer and continue cooking for the remaining 6 minutes.
7. Once the cooking is complete, remove the Breakfast Sausage Balls from the air fryer. Let the sausage balls cool for a few minutes before serving.
8. Serve the **Breakfast Sausage Balls** as a delicious breakfast or brunch option.

Chapter 02: Breakfasts Recipes

Breakfast Sausage Patties

Prep: **10** Min | Cook: **12** Min | Serves: **8 patties**

Ingredient:

- 500g pork sausage meat
- 1 teaspoon dried sage
- 1/2 teaspoon dried thyme
- 1/2 teaspoon garlic powder
- 1/2 teaspoon onion powder
- 1/4 teaspoon salt
- 1/4 teaspoon black pepper
- Cooking spray or oil, for greasing

Instruction:

1. In a large bowl, combine the pork sausage meat, dried sage, dried thyme, garlic powder, onion powder, salt, and black pepper. Mix well until all the ingredients are evenly incorporated.
2. Divide the mixture into 8 equal portions and shape each portion into a patty, approximately 1.5cm thick.
3. Grease Zone 1 and Zone 2 of the air fryer basket with cooking spray or oil.
4. Place the sausage patties in both zones of the air fryer basket, leaving space between each patty.
5. Select Zone 1 and the AIR FRY program. Set the temperature to 180°C and the time to 12 minutes. Select MATCH. Press the START/STOP button to begin cooking.
6. After 6 minutes of cooking, open the air fryer and carefully flip the sausage patties to ensure even browning.
7. Close the air fryer and continue cooking for the remaining 6 minutes or until the sausage patties are cooked through and browned on the outside.
8. Once the cooking is complete, remove the Breakfast Sausage Patties from the air fryer.
9. Let the sausage patties cool for a few minutes before serving.
10. Serve the **Breakfast Sausage Patties** as a delicious addition to your breakfast or brunch. They can be enjoyed on their own, in a sandwich, or alongside other breakfast items.

Cheesy Breakfast Biscuits

Prep: **15** Min | Cook: **10** Min | Serves: **6 biscuits**

Ingredient:

- 225g self-raising flour
- 1/2 teaspoon baking powder
- 1/4 teaspoon salt
- 50g unsalted butter, cold and cubed
- 100g grated cheddar cheese
- 150ml milk
- Cooking spray or oil, for greasing

Instruction:

1. In a large bowl, combine the self-raising flour, baking powder, and salt. Mix well.
2. Add the cold cubed butter to the bowl and rub it into the flour mixture using your fingertips until the mixture resembles breadcrumbs. Stir in the grated cheddar cheese.
3. Gradually add the milk to the bowl, stirring until the mixture comes together to form a soft dough. Be careful not to overmix.
4. Transfer the dough onto a lightly floured surface and gently knead it a few times to bring it together.
5. Roll out the dough to a thickness of approximately 2cm.
6. Using a round cookie cutter or a glass, cut out biscuit shapes from the rolled-out dough and place them in Zone 1 of the air fryer basket, leaving space between each biscuit.
7. Select Zone 1 and the AIR FRY program. Set the temperature to 200°C and the time to 10 minutes. Press the START/STOP button to begin cooking.
8. Once the cooking is complete, remove the Cheesy Breakfast Biscuits from Zone 1. Let the biscuits cool for a few minutes before serving. Serve the **Cheesy Breakfast Biscuits** warm as a delightful addition to your breakfast or brunch.

Chapter 02: Breakfasts Recipes

Cheesy Breakfast Potatoes

Prep: **10** Min | Cook: **20** Min | Serves: **4**

Ingredient:

- 800g potatoes (such as Maris Piper or King Edward), washed and diced into 2cm cubes
- 2 tablespoons olive oil
- 1 teaspoon dried thyme
- 1 teaspoon paprika
- 1/2 teaspoon garlic powder
- 1/2 teaspoon onion powder
- 1/2 teaspoon salt
- 1/4 teaspoon black pepper
- 100g grated cheddar cheese

Instruction:

1. In a large bowl, combine the diced potatoes, olive oil, dried thyme, paprika, garlic powder, onion powder, salt, and black pepper. Toss the potatoes until they are evenly coated with the seasonings.
2. Grease Zone 1 of the air fryer basket with cooking spray or oil.
3. Place the seasoned potatoes in Zone 1 of the air fryer basket, spreading them out in a single layer.
4. Select Zone 1 and the AIR FRY program. Set the temperature to 200°C and the time to 20 minutes. Press the START/STOP button to begin cooking.
5. After 10 minutes of cooking, open the air fryer and carefully toss the potatoes to ensure even browning.
6. Close the air fryer and continue cooking for the remaining 10 minutes or until the potatoes are golden brown and crispy.
7. Once the cooking is complete, remove the Cheesy Breakfast Potatoes from Zone 1.
8. Sprinkle the grated cheddar cheese over the hot potatoes and let it melt for a minute.
9. Serve the **Cheesy Breakfast Potatoes** as a delicious side dish for breakfast or brunch.

Cinnamon French Toast Sticks

Prep: 10 Min | Cook: 10 Min | Serves: 4

Ingredient:

- 8 slices of bread (white or whole wheat), cut into 2cm wide strips
- 3 large eggs
- 120ml milk
- 2 tablespoons granulated sugar
- 1 teaspoon ground cinnamon
- 1/2 teaspoon vanilla extract
- Cooking spray or oil, for greasing

Instruction:

1. In a shallow dish, whisk together the eggs, milk, granulated sugar, ground cinnamon, and vanilla extract until well combined.
2. Grease Zone 1 and Zone 2 of the air fryer basket with cooking spray or oil.
3. Dip each bread strip into the egg mixture, coating both sides evenly, and place them in two zones of the air fryer basket.
4. Select Zone 1 and the AIR FRY program. Set the temperature to 180°C and the time to 10 minutes. Select MATCH. Press the START/STOP button to begin cooking.
5. After 5 minutes of cooking, open the air fryer and carefully flip the French toast sticks to ensure even browning. Close the air fryer and continue cooking for the remaining 5 minutes or until the French toast sticks are golden brown and crispy.
6. Once the cooking is complete, remove the Cinnamon French Toast Sticks from the air fryer.
7. Serve the **Cinnamon French Toast Sticks** warm as a delicious breakfast or brunch treat. You can serve them with maple syrup, powdered sugar, or your favorite dipping sauce.

Chapter 02: Breakfasts Recipes

Cinnamon Roll Twists

Prep: 20 Min | Cook: 10 Min | Serves: 8 twists

Ingredient:

For the dough:
- 250g plain flour
- 2 tablespoons granulated sugar
- 1 teaspoon baking powder
- 1/4 teaspoon salt
- 60g unsalted butter, cold and cubed
- 120ml milk

For the filling:
- 40g unsalted butter, softened
- 3 tablespoons granulated sugar
- 2 teaspoons ground cinnamon

For the glaze:
- 100g icing sugar
- 1-2 tablespoons milk
- 1/2 teaspoon vanilla extract

Instruction:

1. In a large bowl, whisk together the plain flour, granulated sugar, baking powder, and salt. Add the cold cubed butter to the bowl and rub it into the flour mixture using your fingertips until the mixture resembles breadcrumbs.
2. Gradually add the milk to the bowl, stirring until the mixture comes together to form a soft dough. Knead the dough gently for a minute or two until it is smooth.
3. On a lightly floured surface, roll out the dough into a rectangle shape, approximately 30cm x 20cm. Spread the softened butter evenly over the surface of the dough.
4. In a small bowl, mix together the granulated sugar and ground cinnamon. Sprinkle this mixture evenly over the buttered dough.
5. Starting from one of the longer edges, tightly roll up the dough into a log shape. Cut the log into 8 equal portions.
6. Take each portion and twist it a few times, then place it in Zone 1 and Zone 2 of the air fryer basket.
7. Select Zone 1 and the AIR FRY program. Set the temperature to 180°C for 10 minutes. Select MATCH. Press the START/STOP.
8. While the cinnamon roll twists are cooking, prepare the glaze. In a small bowl, whisk together the icing sugar, milk, and vanilla extract until smooth and well combined.
9. Once the cooking is complete, remove the Cinnamon Roll Twists from the air fryer. Drizzle the glaze over the warm twists. Serve the **Cinnamon Roll Twists** as a delicious sweet treat for breakfast.

Egg and Bacon Breakfast Pies

Prep: **15** Min | Cook: **15** Min | Serves: **4 pies**

Ingredient:

- 4 sheets of ready-rolled puff pastry, each measuring approximately 20cm x 20cm
- 4 large eggs
- 4 slices of bacon, cooked and chopped
- 50g grated cheddar cheese
- Salt and pepper, to taste
- 1 tablespoon chopped fresh parsley (optional)
- Cooking spray or oil, for greasing

Instruction:

1. Grease Zone 1 and Zone 2 of the air fryer basket with cooking spray or oil.
2. Place one sheet of puff pastry in both zones of the air fryer basket. Gently press the pastry into the corners and along the sides of the basket.
3. Crack an egg onto the center of the pastry sheet.
4. Sprinkle some chopped bacon, grated cheddar cheese, salt, and pepper over the egg.
5. Fold the corners of the pastry sheet over the egg and filling, creating a square-shaped pie. You can tuck any excess pastry underneath to seal it.
6. Select Zone 1 and the AIR FRY program. Set the temperature to 180°C and the time to 15 minutes. Select MATCH. Press the START/STOP button to begin cooking.
7. Once the cooking is complete, remove the Egg and Bacon Breakfast Pies from the air fryer.
8. Sprinkle some chopped fresh parsley over the pies, if desired, for added flavor and garnish.
9. Serve the **Egg and Bacon Breakfast Pies** warm as a delicious and satisfying breakfast or brunch option.

Chapter 02: Breakfasts Recipes

Egg and Bacon Muffins

Prep: **10** Min | Cook: **12** Min | Serves: **4 muffins**

Ingredient:

- 4 English muffins, split
- 4 slices of bacon
- 4 large eggs
- Salt and pepper, to taste
- 2 tablespoons butter, softened
- Optional toppings: sliced cheese, tomato, spinach, etc.

Instruction:

1. Place the bacon slices in Zone 1 of the air fryer basket. Select Zone 1 and the AIR FRY program. Set the temperature to 180°C and the time to 6 minutes. Press the START/STOP button to begin cooking. Flip the bacon halfway through the cooking time to ensure it cooks evenly.
2. While the bacon is cooking, spread the softened butter on the cut sides of the English muffins.
3. Once the bacon is cooked, remove it from Zone 1 and set it aside.
4. Place the English muffin halves, cut side down, in Zone 1 of the air fryer basket.
5. Crack an egg into each muffin half. Season with salt and pepper.
6. Select Zone 1 and the AIR FRY program. Set the temperature to 180°C and the time to 6 minutes. Press the START/STOP button to begin cooking.
7. While the eggs and muffins are cooking, chop the cooked bacon into small pieces.
8. Once the cooking is complete, remove the Egg and Bacon Muffins from Zone 1.
9. Place the chopped bacon on top of the eggs in each muffin half.
10. Optionally, add any desired toppings such as sliced cheese, tomato, or spinach. Sandwich the English muffin halves together to form a complete muffin.
11. Serve the **Egg and Bacon Muffins** warm as a delicious breakfast or brunch option.

Egg and Spinach Breakfast Cups

Prep: **15** Min | Cook: **10** Min | Serves: **4 cups**

Ingredient:

- 4 slices of bread
- 4 large eggs
- 100g fresh spinach, roughly chopped
- 50g grated cheddar cheese
- Salt and pepper, to taste
- Cooking spray or oil, for greasing

...▶ *Instruction:*

1. Grease Zone 1 of the air fryer basket with cooking spray or oil.
2. Flatten the bread slices using a rolling pin. Press each slice into Zone 1 of the air fryer basket, forming a cup shape. Ensure the bread is securely pressed against the sides of the basket.
3. Place a portion of chopped spinach in each bread cup.
4. Crack an egg into each bread cup, on top of the spinach.
5. Sprinkle grated cheddar cheese over the eggs. Season with salt and pepper.
6. Select Zone 1 and the AIR FRY program. Set the temperature to 180°C and the time to 10 minutes. Press the START/STOP button to begin cooking.
7. Once the cooking is complete, remove the Egg and Spinach Breakfast Cups from Zone 1.
8. Serve the **Egg and Spinach Breakfast Cups** warm as a nutritious and flavorful breakfast or brunch option.

Chapter 02: Breakfasts Recipes

Egg and Veggie Breakfast Wraps

Prep: **15** Min | Cook: **10** Min | Serves: **4 wraps**

Ingredient:

- 4 large tortilla wraps
- 4 large eggs
- 1 red bell pepper, sliced
- 1 red onion, sliced
- 100g mushrooms, sliced
- 50g baby spinach leaves
- 50g grated cheddar cheese
- Salt and pepper, to taste
- Cooking spray or oil, for greasing

...▶ *Instruction:*

1. Grease Zone 1 and Zone 2 of the air fryer basket with cooking spray or oil.
2. In Zone 1, place the sliced bell pepper, red onion, and mushrooms. In Zone 2, place the tortilla wraps. Select Zone 1 and the AIR FRY program. Set the temperature to 180°C and the time to 8 minutes. Select MATCH. Press the START/STOP button to begin cooking.
3. After 2 minutes cooking, remove the tortilla wraps from Zone 2. Close the air fryer and continue cooking sliced bell pepper for the remaining 6 minutes.
4. While the veggies and wraps are cooking, crack eggs into a small bowl. In a frying pan, heat a medium amount of oil. Pour the crack egg into the pan. Season with salt and pepper.
5. Once the cooking is complete, remove the veggies and eggs from the air fryer.
6. Assemble the wraps by placing a handful of baby spinach leaves on each tortilla wrap. Divide the cooked sliced bell pepper evenly among the wraps, placing them on top of the spinach.
7. Place cooked eggs on top of the veggies in each wrap. Sprinkle grated cheddar cheese over the eggs. Roll up the wraps tightly, tucking in the sides as you go.
8. Serve the **Egg and Veggie Breakfast Wraps** warm as a delicious and satisfying breakfast or brunch option.

Egg Muffins

Prep: **10** Min | Cook: **12** Min | Serves: **6 muffins**

Ingredient:

- 6 large eggs
- 50g grated cheddar cheese
- 50g diced cooked ham
- 50g diced bell peppers
- 50g diced onions
- Salt and pepper, to taste
- Vegetable oil, for greasing

Instruction:

1. In a mixing bowl, crack the eggs and whisk them until well beaten. Season with salt and pepper.
2. Grease the air fryer muffin cups with vegetable oil to prevent sticking.
3. Divide the diced ham, bell peppers, and onions evenly among the 6 muffin cups.
4. Pour the beaten eggs into each muffin cup, filling them about three-quarters full.
5. Sprinkle grated cheddar cheese over the top of each egg muffin.
6. Place muffin cups in Zone 1. Select Zone 1 and the BAKE program. Set the temperature to 180°C and the time to 12 minutes. Press the START/STOP button to begin cooking.
7. Once cooked, carefully remove the egg muffins from the air fryer and let them cool for a few minutes.
8. Serve the **Egg Muffins** warm as a delicious breakfast or snack.

Chapter 02: Breakfasts Recipes

Egg-in-a-Hole

Prep: **5** Min | Cook: **8** Min | Serves: **2**

Ingredient:

- 2 slices of bread
- 2 large eggs
- 20g butter
- Salt and pepper, to taste

Instruction:

1. Grease Zone 1 of the air fryer basket with cooking spray or oil.
2. Using a round cookie cutter or the rim of a glass, cut out a hole in the center of each bread slice. Set aside the bread circles.
3. Spread butter on both sides of each bread slice, including the cut-out hole pieces.
4. Place the bread slices in Zone 1 of the air fryer basket. Select Zone 1 and the AIR FRY program. Set the temperature to 180°C and the time to 4 minutes. Press the START/STOP button to begin toasting the bread.
5. While the bread is toasting, crack an egg into a small bowl, taking care not to break the yolk. Repeat with the second egg.
6. After 4 minutes of toasting, remove the air fryer basket and carefully flip the bread slices over.
7. Pour one cracked egg into the hole of each bread slice. Season with salt and pepper.
8. Place the bread circles on the side of the air fryer basket. These will also cook alongside the eggs.
9. Select Zone 1 and the AIR FRY program. Set the temperature to 180°C and the time to 4 minutes. Press the START/STOP button to begin cooking the eggs and the bread circles.
10. Once the cooking is complete, remove the air fryer basket.
11. Serve the **Egg-in-a-Hole** warm with the toasted bread circles on the side. You can enjoy them as is or pair them with additional sides like bacon, sausage, or grilled tomatoes.

English Muffin Breakfast Sandwiches

Prep: **10** Min | Cook: **8** Min | Serves: **2 sandwiches**

Ingredient:

- 2 English muffins, split
- 4 slices of bacon
- 2 large eggs
- 50g cheddar cheese, grated
- 1 tablespoon butter
- Salt and pepper, to taste

Instruction:

1. In Zone 1, place the bacon slices. Select Zone 1 and the AIR FRY program. Set the temperature to 180°C and the time to 8 minutes. Press the START/STOP button to begin cooking the bacon until crispy.
2. Spread butter on the cut sides of each English muffin half.
3. Place the English muffin halves, cut side up, in Zone 2 of the air fryer basket. Select Zone 2 and the AIR FRY program. Set the temperature to 180°C and the time to 4 minutes. Press the START/STOP button to begin toasting the English muffins.
4. In a frying pan, heat a medium amount of oil. Pour one cracked egg into the pan. Season with salt and pepper. Cook for 3 minutes until desired doneness.
5. Assemble the sandwiches by placing a slice of bacon on the bottom half of each English muffin. Top with a cooked egg and sprinkle grated cheddar cheese over the eggs.
6. Place the top halves of the English muffins on top of the cheese.
7. Return the assembled sandwiches to Zone 2 of the air fryer basket. Melt the cheese and warm the sandwiches for 1 minute.
8. Serve the **English Muffin Breakfast Sandwiches** warm as a delicious breakfast or brunch option.

Chapter 02: Breakfasts Recipes

Fruit and Nut Granola

Prep: **10** Min | Cook: **20** Min | Serves: **4-6**

Ingredient:

- 200g old-fashioned oats
- 50g mixed nuts (such as almonds, walnuts, and pecans), roughly chopped
- 50g seeds (such as pumpkin seeds and sunflower seeds)
- 2 tablespoons honey or maple syrup
- 2 tablespoons vegetable oil
- 1 teaspoon vanilla extract
- 1/2 teaspoon ground cinnamon
- A pinch of salt
- 50g dried fruit (such as raisins, dried cranberries, or chopped dried apricots)

Instruction:

1. In a large bowl, combine the oats, mixed nuts, seeds, honey (or maple syrup), vegetable oil, vanilla extract, cinnamon, and a pinch of salt. Stir well to ensure that the oats and nuts are well coated with the honey and oil.
2. Spread the granola mixture evenly in zone 1 of the air fryer basket.
3. Select Zone 1 and the BAKE program. Set the temperature to 160°C and the time to 15-20 minutes or until the granola is golden brown and crispy. Press the START/STOP button to begin cooking the granola.
4. Shake the basket or stir the granola halfway through the cooking time to ensure even browning.
5. Once the granola is cooked and still warm, stir in the dried fruit.
6. Allow the granola to cool completely in the basket or on a baking sheet. This will help it get crunchier.
7. Once cooled, transfer the granola to an airtight container. It can be stored at room temperature for up to 2 weeks.
8. Enjoy your homemade **Fruit and Nut Granola** with yogurt, milk, or as a crunchy topping for smoothie bowls.

Hash Browns

Prep: **15** Min | Cook: **20** Min | Serves: **4 hash browns**

Ingredient:

- 500g potatoes, peeled and grated
- 1 small onion, finely chopped
- 2 tablespoons plain flour
- 1 teaspoon salt
- 1/2 teaspoon ground black pepper
- 2 tablespoons vegetable oil

Instruction:

1. In a clean kitchen towel, place the grated potatoes and squeeze out any excess moisture.
2. In a large mixing bowl, combine the grated potatoes, chopped onion, plain flour, salt, and ground black pepper. Mix well to evenly distribute the ingredients.
3. Grease Zone 1 of the air fryer basket with cooking spray or oil.
4. Divide the potato mixture into 4 equal portions. Shape each portion into a round hash brown patty, about 1 cm thick.
5. Place the hash brown patties in Zone 1 of the air fryer basket.
6. Select Zone 1 and the ROAST program. Set the temperature to 200°C and the time to 10 minutes. Press the START/STOP button to begin cooking the hash browns.
7. After 10 minutes, open the air fryer and carefully flip the hash brown patties using tongs or a spatula. Close the air fryer and continue cooking for the remaining 10 minutes.
8. Once the cooking is complete, remove the hash browns from the air fryer and let them cool slightly before serving.
9. Serve the **Hash Browns** as a delicious side dish for breakfast or brunch. They pair well with eggs, bacon, or sausages.

Chapter 02: Breakfasts Recipes

Sausage and Egg Breakfast Burritos

Prep: **15** Min | Cook: **20** Min | Serves: **4 burritos**

Ingredient:

- 4 large eggs
- 4 sausage links, cooked and sliced
- 1 tablespoon butter
- 1 small onion, finely chopped
- 1 small red bell pepper, finely chopped
- 4 tortilla wraps
- 50g cheddar cheese, grated
- Salt and pepper, to taste

Instruction:

1. In a bowl, whisk the eggs until well beaten. Set aside.
2. In a skillet over medium heat, melt the butter. Add the chopped onion and red bell pepper. Sauté until the vegetables are softened.
3. Pour the beaten eggs into the skillet with the sautéed vegetables. Cook, stirring occasionally, until the eggs are scrambled and cooked through. Season with salt and pepper to taste.
4. Lay out the tortilla wraps on a clean surface. Divide the scrambled eggs, cooked sausage slices, and grated cheddar cheese equally among the tortillas.
5. Roll up the tortillas, folding in the sides as you go, to form burritos.
6. Grease Zone 1 of the air fryer basket with cooking spray or oil.
7. Place the breakfast burritos in Zone 1 of the air fryer basket.
8. Select Zone 1 and the AIR FRY program. Set the temperature to 180°C and the time to 10 minutes. Press the START/STOP.
9. After 10 minutes, open the air fryer and carefully flip the breakfast burritos using tongs or a spatula. Close the air fryer and continue cooking for another 10 minutes.
10. Once the cooking is complete, remove the breakfast burritos from the air fryer and let them cool slightly before serving.
11. Serve the **Sausage and Egg Breakfast Burritos** as a delicious and satisfying breakfast option.

BBQ Chicken Drumsticks

Prep: **10** Min | Cook: **25** Min | Serves: **4**

Ingredient:

- 8 chicken drumsticks
- 150g BBQ sauce
- 2 tablespoons olive oil
- 1 tablespoon Worcestershire sauce
- 1 tablespoon honey
- 1 teaspoon smoked paprika
- 1 teaspoon garlic powder
- Salt and pepper, to taste
- Chopped fresh parsley, for garnish (optional)

Instruction:

1. In a bowl, whisk together the BBQ sauce, olive oil, Worcestershire sauce, honey, smoked paprika, garlic powder, salt, and pepper.
2. Place the chicken drumsticks in a large ziplock bag or a bowl. Pour the BBQ sauce mixture over the drumsticks, ensuring they are well coated. Marinate for at least 30 minutes, or overnight in the refrigerator for better flavor.
3. Grease Zone 1 of the air fryer basket with cooking spray or oil.
4. Place the marinated chicken drumsticks in Zone 1 of the air fryer basket, leaving space between them for proper air circulation.
5. Select Zone 1 and the AIR FRY program. Set the temperature to 180°C and the time to 25 minutes. Press the START/STOP button to begin cooking the chicken drumsticks.
6. After 15 minutes of cooking, open the air fryer and carefully flip the chicken drumsticks using tongs or a spatula. Close the air fryer and continue cooking for the remaining 10 minutes.
7. Once cooked, remove the BBQ chicken drumsticks from the air fryer and let them rest for a few minutes. Garnish with chopped fresh parsley, if desired, before serving.
8. Serve the **BBQ Chicken Drumsticks** as a flavorful main dish, accompanied by your favorite sides like coleslaw, corn on the cob, or potato wedges.

Chapter 03: Poultry

Buffalo Chicken Wings

Prep: **10** Min | Cook: **25** Min | Serves: **4**

Ingredient:

- 800g chicken wings
- 60g unsalted butter
- 100g hot sauce (e.g., Frank's RedHot)
- 1 tablespoon white vinegar
- 1/2 teaspoon Worcestershire sauce
- 1/2 teaspoon garlic powder
- 1/2 teaspoon paprika
- Salt and pepper, to taste
- Blue cheese dressing or ranch dressing, for serving
- Celery sticks, for serving

Instruction:

1. In a small saucepan, melt the butter over low heat. Add the hot sauce, white vinegar, Worcestershire sauce, garlic powder, paprika, salt, and pepper. Stir until well combined and heated through. Remove from heat.
2. Grease Zone 1 and Zone 2 of the air fryer basket with cooking spray or oil.
3. Place the chicken wings in both zones of the air fryer basket, leaving space between them for proper air circulation.
4. Select Zone 1 and the AIR FRY program. Set the temperature to 200°C and the time to 25 minutes. Select MATCH. Press the START/STOP button to begin cooking the chicken wings.
5. After 15 minutes of cooking, open the air fryer and carefully flip the chicken wings using tongs or a spatula. Close the air fryer and continue cooking for the remaining 10 minutes or until the wings are crispy and golden brown.
6. Once cooked, transfer the chicken wings to a large bowl. Pour the prepared buffalo sauce over the wings and toss to coat evenly.
7. Serve the **Buffalo Chicken Wings** with blue cheese dressing or ranch dressing for dipping. Serve with celery sticks on the side.

Chicken and Vegetable Skewers

Prep: **20** Min | Cook: **15** Min | Serves: **4 skewers**

Ingredient:

- 400g boneless, skinless chicken breast, cut into 2.5cm pieces
- 1 red bell pepper, cut into 2.5cm pieces
- 1 green bell pepper, cut into 2.5cm pieces
- 1 red onion, cut into 2.5cm pieces
- 8 cherry tomatoes
- 2 tablespoons olive oil
- 2 tablespoons lemon juice
- 2 cloves garlic, minced
- 1 teaspoon dried mixed herbs
- Salt and pepper, to taste
- Wooden skewers, soaked in water for 30 minutes

Instruction:

1. In a bowl, combine the olive oil, lemon juice, minced garlic, dried mixed herbs, salt, and pepper. Mix well.
2. Add the chicken pieces to the bowl and toss to coat them evenly with the marinade. Allow the chicken to marinate for at least 10 minutes.
3. Thread the marinated chicken pieces, bell peppers, red onion, and cherry tomatoes onto the soaked wooden skewers, alternating the ingredients.
4. Grease Zone 1 of the air fryer basket with cooking spray or oil.
5. Place the chicken and vegetable skewers in Zone 1 of the air fryer basket, making sure they are not too crowded.
6. Select Zone 1 and the AIR FRY program. Set the temperature to 200°C and the time to 15 minutes. Press the START/STOP button to begin cooking the skewers.
7. After 7 minutes of cooking, open the air fryer and carefully flip the skewers using tongs or a spatula. Close the air fryer and continue cooking for the remaining 8 minutes or until the chicken is cooked through and the vegetables are tender.
8. Serve the **Chicken and Vegetable Skewers** as a delicious and healthy main course option, accompanied by a side salad or rice.

Chapter 03: Poultry

Chicken Burgers

Prep: **15** Min | Cook: **12** Min | Serves: **4 burgers**

Ingredient:

- 500g ground chicken
- 1 small onion, finely chopped
- 2 cloves garlic, minced
- 1 teaspoon dried thyme
- 1 teaspoon dried rosemary
- 1/2 teaspoon paprika
- 1/2 teaspoon salt
- 1/4 teaspoon black pepper
- 4 burger buns
- Lettuce leaves
- Sliced tomatoes
- Sliced red onion
- Pickles
- Condiments of your choice (mayonnaise, ketchup, mustard)

Instruction:

1. In a mixing bowl, combine the ground chicken, chopped onion, minced garlic, dried thyme, dried rosemary, paprika, salt, and black pepper. Mix well until all the ingredients are evenly incorporated.
2. Divide the mixture into four equal portions and shape them into burger patties.
3. Grease Zone 1 of the air fryer basket with cooking spray or oil.
4. Place the chicken burger patties in Zone 1 of the air fryer basket, leaving space between them for proper air circulation.
5. Select Zone 1 and the AIR FRY program. Set the temperature to 200°C and the time to 12 minutes. Press the START/STOP button to begin cooking the burgers.
6. After 6 minutes of cooking, open the air fryer and carefully flip the burgers using tongs or a spatula. Close the air fryer and continue cooking for the remaining 6 minutes or until the burgers are cooked through and reach an internal temperature of 75°C.
7. While the burgers are cooking, prepare your burger buns and toppings. Toast the burger buns if desired.
8. Once cooked, remove the chicken burgers from the air fryer and assemble them on the burger buns with lettuce leaves, sliced tomatoes, sliced red onion, pickles, and your choice of condiments.
9. Serve the **Chicken Burgers** immediately with your favorite sides, such as fries or coleslaw.

Chicken Caesar Pizza

Prep: 20 Min | Cook: 10 Min | Serves: 1 pizza

Ingredient:

For the Pizza Dough:
- 250g strong white bread flour
- 1/2 teaspoon salt
- 1/2 teaspoon instant yeast
- 1 tablespoon olive oil

For the Toppings:
- 200g cooked chicken breast, shredded
- 4 tablespoons Caesar dressing
- 120g shredded mozzarella cheese
- 25g grated Parmesan cheese
- 2 tablespoons chopped fresh parsley
- Freshly ground black pepper, to taste
- Fresh lettuce leaves, torn
- Cherry tomatoes, halved

Instruction:

1. Mix the flour and salt in a bowl. Dissolve the yeast in warm water, then add it along with the olive oil to the flour mixture. Mix until a dough forms.
2. Knead the dough on a floured surface for 5 minutes until smooth. Cover and let it rest for 10 minutes.
3. Roll out the dough into a 25cm round pizza shape on a floured surface. Place it on a parchment paper-lined tray that fits Zone 1 of the air fryer basket.
4. Spread Caesar dressing evenly on the dough, leaving a small border. Add shredded chicken, mozzarella cheese, and grated Parmesan cheese.
5. Place the pizza in Zone 1 of the air fryer basket, ensuring it fits without touching the sides.
6. Select Zone 1 and the AIR FRY program. Set the temperature to 200°C for 10 minutes. Press the START/STOP.
7. After 5 minutes, open the air fryer and sprinkle chopped parsley and black pepper over the pizza. Close and continue cooking for the remaining 5 minutes.
8. Remove the **Chicken Caesar Pizza** from the air fryer and let it cool for a few minutes. Top with torn lettuce leaves and halved cherry tomatoes.

Chapter 03: Poultry

Chicken Caesar Salad

Prep: 15 Min | Cook: 12 Min | Serves: 2

Ingredient:

For the Chicken:
- 2 boneless, skinless chicken breasts (about 300g)
- 1 tablespoon olive oil
- 1 teaspoon garlic powder
- 1/2 teaspoon salt
- 1/4 teaspoon black pepper

For the Salad:
- 2 romaine lettuce hearts, washed and chopped
- 50g grated Parmesan cheese
- Caesar dressing (store-bought or homemade)
- Croutons (optional)

Instruction:

1. In a bowl, combine the olive oil, garlic powder, salt, and black pepper. Brush the chicken breasts with the mixture, ensuring they are evenly coated.
2. Place the chicken breasts in Zone 1 of the air fryer basket.
3. Select Zone 1 and the AIR FRY program. Set the temperature to 200°C and the time to 12 minutes. Press the START/STOP button to begin cooking the chicken.
4. While the chicken is cooking, prepare the salad. In a large bowl, combine the chopped romaine lettuce and grated Parmesan cheese.
5. Once the chicken is cooked, remove it from the air fryer and let it rest for a few minutes. Slice the chicken breasts into thin strips.
6. Add the sliced chicken to the bowl of lettuce and Parmesan cheese. Drizzle Caesar dressing over the salad to taste and toss well to combine.
7. Divide the Chicken Caesar Salad into two serving plates. If desired, sprinkle croutons over the salad for added crunch.
8. Serve the **Chicken Caesar Salad** immediately as a refreshing and satisfying meal.

Chicken Caesar Wraps

Prep: **20** Min | Cook: **12** Min | Serves: **2 wraps**

Ingredient:

For the Chicken:
- 2 boneless, skinless chicken breasts (about 300g total)
- 1 tablespoon olive oil
- 1 teaspoon garlic powder
- 1/2 teaspoon salt
- 1/4 teaspoon black pepper

For the Wraps:
- 2 large tortilla wraps
- 4 tablespoons Caesar dressing
- 100g romaine lettuce, washed and chopped
- 50g grated Parmesan cheese
- Cherry tomatoes, halved
- Freshly ground black pepper, to taste

Instruction:

1. In a bowl, combine the olive oil, garlic powder, salt, and black pepper. Brush the chicken breasts with the mixture, ensuring they are evenly coated.
2. Place the chicken breasts in Zone 1 of the air fryer basket.
3. Select Zone 1 and the AIR FRY program. Set the temperature to 200°C and the time to 12 minutes. Press the START/STOP button to begin cooking the chicken.
4. While the chicken is cooking, prepare the wraps. Spread 2 tablespoons of Caesar dressing onto each tortilla wrap, leaving a small border around the edges.
5. In a bowl, combine the chopped romaine lettuce, grated Parmesan cheese, and cherry tomatoes. Toss well to mix.
6. Once the chicken is cooked, remove it from the air fryer and let it rest for a few minutes. Slice the chicken breasts into thin strips.
7. Place the sliced chicken on top of the Caesar dressing on each wrap. Add a generous amount of the lettuce mixture on top. Season with freshly ground black pepper.
8. Fold the sides of the wraps inward and roll them tightly to form a wrap shape. Cut each wrap in half diagonally to create two portions. Serve the **Chicken Caesar Wraps** immediately as a delicious and convenient meal.

Chapter 03: Poultry

Chicken Cordon Bleu

Prep: **15** Min | Cook: **20** Min | Serves: **2**

Ingredient:

- 2 boneless, skinless chicken breasts (about 300g)
- 4 thin slices of ham
- 100g grated Gruyère cheese (or Swiss cheese)
- 1/2 teaspoon garlic powder
- 1/2 teaspoon dried thyme
- 1/2 teaspoon salt
- 1/4 teaspoon black pepper
- 1 egg, beaten
- 50g breadcrumbs

Instruction:

1. Flatten the chicken breasts to an even thickness. You can do this by placing them between two sheets of plastic wrap and pounding gently with a meat mallet or rolling pin.
2. Sprinkle the flattened chicken breasts with garlic powder, dried thyme, salt, and black pepper.
3. Place 2 slices of ham on each chicken breast, followed by half of the grated Gruyère cheese. Roll up the chicken breasts tightly.
4. Dip each rolled chicken breast in the beaten egg, ensuring it is coated all over.
5. Roll the chicken breasts in breadcrumbs, pressing lightly to adhere the breadcrumbs to the surface.
6. Place the chicken breasts in Zone 1 of the air fryer basket.
7. Select Zone 1 and the AIR FRY program. Set the temperature to 200°C and the time to 20 minutes. Press the START/STOP button to begin cooking the chicken.
8. After 10 minutes of cooking, open the air fryer and flip the chicken breasts. This will ensure even browning on all sides. Close and continue cooking for the remaining 10 minutes.
9. Once the chicken is cooked and golden brown, remove it from the air fryer and let it rest for a few minutes before slicing.
10. Slice each chicken breast into medallions and serve hot as a delicious **Chicken Cordon Bleu**.

Chicken Drumsticks

Prep: **10** Min | Cook: **30** Min | Serves: **4**

Ingredient:

- 8 chicken drumsticks (about 800g total)
- 1 tablespoon olive oil
- 1 teaspoon paprika
- 1 teaspoon garlic powder
- 1/2 teaspoon dried thyme
- 1/2 teaspoon salt
- 1/4 teaspoon black pepper

Instruction:

1. In a bowl, combine the olive oil, paprika, garlic powder, dried thyme, salt, and black pepper. Mix well to create a marinade.
2. Pat the chicken drumsticks dry with paper towels. Place them in a separate bowl or zip-top bag.
3. Pour the marinade over the chicken drumsticks, ensuring they are evenly coated. Massage the marinade into the drumsticks for better flavor penetration.
4. Place the chicken drumsticks in both zones of the air fryer basket.
5. Select Zone 1 and the AIR FRY program. Set the temperature to 200°C and the time to 30 minutes. Select MATCH. Press the START/STOP button to begin cooking the drumsticks.
6. After 15 minutes of cooking, open the air fryer and flip the drumsticks. This will help them cook evenly. Close and continue cooking for the remaining 15 minutes.
7. Once the chicken drumsticks are cooked through and crispy on the outside, remove them from the air fryer and let them rest for a few minutes.
8. Serve the **Chicken Drumsticks** hot as a flavorful and tender main dish. They pair well with your favorite dipping sauces or served alongside a fresh salad or vegetables.

Chapter 03: Poultry

Chicken Enchiladas

Prep: **20** Min | Cook: **25** Min | Serves: **4**

Ingredient:

- 2 boneless, skinless chicken breasts (about 400g)
- 1 tablespoon olive oil
- 1 onion, finely chopped
- 2 cloves of garlic, minced
- 1 teaspoon ground cumin
- 1 teaspoon chili powder
- 1/2 teaspoon dried oregano
- 1/2 teaspoon salt
- 1/4 teaspoon black pepper
- 8 small flour tortillas
- 200g grated cheddar cheese
- 200g enchilada sauce (store-bought or homemade)
- Fresh cilantro leaves, for garnish (optional)

Instruction:

1. In a saucepan over medium heat, warm the olive oil. Add the chopped onion and minced garlic, and sauté until the onion is translucent.
2. Add the ground cumin, chili powder, dried oregano, salt, and black pepper to the saucepan. Stir well to coat the onion and garlic with the spices.
3. Add the chicken breasts to the saucepan and cook until they are browned on the outside. Remove the chicken from the saucepan and let it cool slightly.
4. Shred the cooked chicken using two forks. Set aside.
5. In Zone 1 of the air fryer basket, place a tortilla. Spoon a portion of the shredded chicken onto the tortilla, followed by a sprinkle of grated cheddar cheese. Roll up the tortilla tightly and place it seam-side down.
6. Select Zone 1 and the AIR FRY program. Set the temperature to 200°C and the time to 15 minutes. Press the START/STOP button to begin cooking the enchiladas.
7. After 15 minutes, pour the enchilada sauce over the cooked enchiladas in Zone 1. Sprinkle the remaining grated cheddar cheese on top. Close the air fryer and continue cooking for an additional 10 minutes or until the cheese is melted and bubbly.
8. Serve the **Chicken Enchiladas** hot as a flavorful and satisfying meal. They pair well with sour cream, guacamole, or salsa.

Chicken Fajitas

Prep: **15** Min | Cook: **20** Min | Serves: **4**

Ingredient:

- 2 boneless, skinless chicken breasts (about 400g)
- 1 red bell pepper, sliced
- 1 green bell pepper, sliced
- 1 onion, sliced
- 2 tablespoons olive oil
- 1 teaspoon mild chili powder
- 1 teaspoon ground cumin
- 1/2 teaspoon smoked paprika
- 1/2 teaspoon garlic powder
- 1/2 teaspoon salt
- 1/4 teaspoon black pepper
- Juice of 1 lime
- 8 small flour tortillas
- Optional toppings: natural yogurt, sliced avocado, grated cheese, fresh coriander

Instruction:

1. Slice the chicken breasts into thin strips. Set aside.
2. In a bowl, combine the mild chili powder, ground cumin, smoked paprika, garlic powder, salt, black pepper, and lime juice. Mix well to create a marinade.
3. Place the chicken strips, sliced bell peppers, and onion in the bowl with the marinade. Toss until all the ingredients are coated.
4. In Zone 1 of the air fryer basket, place the marinated chicken, bell peppers, and onion. Drizzle with 1 tablespoon of olive oil.
5. Select Zone 1 and the AIR FRY program. Set the temperature to 200°C and the time to 20 minutes. Press the START/STOP button to begin cooking the fajitas.
6. Halfway through the cooking time, open the air fryer and give the ingredients a stir for even cooking. Close and continue cooking for the remaining time.
7. While the fajitas are cooking, warm the tortillas in a dry pan or in the microwave.
8. Once the fajitas are cooked and the chicken is tender, remove them from the air fryer.
9. Serve the **Chicken Fajitas** hot, with warm tortillas and your choice of toppings such as natural yogurt, sliced avocado, grated cheese, and fresh coriander.

Chapter 03: Poultry

Chicken Fritters

Prep: **15** Min | Cook: **10** Min | Serves: **4**

Ingredient:

- 500g boneless, skinless chicken breasts
- 1 small onion, finely chopped
- 2 cloves garlic, minced
- 1 small carrot, grated
- 2 tablespoons chopped fresh parsley
- 1 teaspoon dried thyme
- 1 teaspoon paprika
- 1/2 teaspoon salt
- 1/4 teaspoon black pepper
- 2 eggs
- 100g breadcrumbs
- Cooking spray or oil, for greasing

Instruction:

1. Cut the chicken breasts into small pieces and place them in a food processor. Pulse until the chicken is finely chopped but not pureed.
2. In a mixing bowl, combine the finely chopped chicken, chopped onion, minced garlic, grated carrot, chopped parsley, dried thyme, paprika, salt, and black pepper. Mix well to combine.
3. In a separate bowl, lightly beat the eggs.
4. Shape the chicken mixture into small fritters, about 5cm in diameter. Dip each fritter into the beaten eggs, then coat it with breadcrumbs.
5. Grease the air fryer basket with cooking spray or a small amount of oil to prevent sticking.
6. In Zone 1 and Zone 2 of the air fryer basket, place the chicken fritters in a single layer. Make sure not to overcrowd the basket.
7. Select Zone 1 and the AIR FRY program. Set the temperature to 200°C and the time to 10 minutes. Select MATCH. Press the START/STOP button to begin cooking the fritters.
8. After 5 minutes, open the air fryer and flip the fritters to ensure even cooking. Close and continue cooking for the remaining 5 minutes.
9. Serve the **Chicken Fritters** hot as a delicious appetizer or main dish. They can be enjoyed on their own or with a dipping sauce of your choice.

Chicken Goujons

Prep: **15** Min | Cook: **12** Min | Serves: **4**

Ingredient:

- 500g boneless, skinless chicken breasts
- 100g plain flour
- 2 eggs, beaten
- 150g breadcrumbs
- 1 teaspoon paprika
- 1/2 teaspoon garlic powder
- 1/2 teaspoon salt
- 1/4 teaspoon black pepper
- Cooking spray or oil, for greasing

Instruction:

1. Cut the chicken breasts into long, thin strips, about 1.5cm wide.
2. In a shallow dish, combine the plain flour, paprika, garlic powder, salt, and black pepper.
3. Place the beaten eggs in a separate shallow dish.
4. In another dish, mix the breadcrumbs with a pinch of salt and black pepper. Dip each chicken strip into the flour mixture, coating it evenly. Shake off any excess flour.
5. Next, dip the floured chicken strip into the beaten eggs, ensuring it is coated thoroughly.
6. Finally, roll the chicken strip in the breadcrumb mixture, pressing gently to adhere the breadcrumbs to the chicken.
7. In Zone 1 and Zone 2 of the air fryer basket, place the coated chicken goujons in a single layer.
8. Select Zone 1 and the AIR FRY program. Set the temperature to 200°C for 12 minutes. Select MATCH. Press the START/STOP.
9. After 6 minutes, open the air fryer and flip the goujons to ensure even cooking. Close and continue cooking for the remaining 6 minutes.
10. Serve the **Chicken Goujons** hot with your favorite dipping sauce, such as ketchup or mayonnaise. They make a delicious appetizer or main dish.

Chapter 03: Poultry

Chicken Kebabs

Prep: **20** Min | Cook: **15** Min | Serves: **4**

Ingredient:

- 500g boneless, skinless chicken breasts
- 1 red bell pepper
- 1 green bell pepper
- 1 red onion
- 2 tablespoons olive oil
- 2 cloves garlic, minced
- 1 teaspoon paprika
- 1 teaspoon ground cumin
- 1/2 teaspoon ground coriander
- 1/2 teaspoon turmeric
- 1/2 teaspoon salt
- 1/4 teaspoon black pepper
- Juice of 1 lemon
- Cooking spray or oil, for greasing

Instruction:

1. Cut the chicken breasts into bite-sized pieces, about 2.5cm cubes.
2. Slice the red and green bell peppers and red onion into similar-sized pieces.
3. In a bowl, combine the olive oil, minced garlic, paprika, ground cumin, ground coriander, turmeric, salt, black pepper, and lemon juice. Mix well to create a marinade.
4. Add the chicken pieces to the marinade and toss until well-coated. Let it marinate for about 10 minutes.
5. Skewer the marinated chicken pieces, alternating with the bell peppers and red onion.
6. In Zone 1 of the air fryer basket, place the chicken kebabs in a single layer. Make sure not to overcrowd the basket.
7. Select Zone 1 and the AIR FRY program. Set the temperature to 200°C and the time to 15 minutes. Press the START/STOP button to begin cooking the kebabs.
8. After 7 minutes, open the air fryer and flip the kebabs to ensure even cooking. Close and continue cooking for the remaining 8 minutes.
9. Once the chicken is cooked through and the vegetables are tender, remove the kebabs from the air fryer.
10. Serve the **Chicken Kebabs** hot with a side of rice, couscous, or salad. They can be enjoyed as a main dish or as part of a barbecue spread.

Chicken Kiev

Prep: **30** Min | Cook: **20** Min | Serves: **4**

Ingredient:

- 4 boneless, skinless chicken breasts
- 100g unsalted butter, softened
- 2 cloves garlic, minced
- 2 tablespoons chopped fresh parsley
- 1 tablespoon lemon juice
- 1/2 teaspoon salt
- 1/4 teaspoon black pepper
- 100g plain flour
- 2 eggs, beaten
- 150g breadcrumbs
- Cooking spray or oil, for greasing

Instruction:

1. In a bowl, combine the softened butter, minced garlic, chopped parsley, lemon juice, salt, and black pepper. Mix well.
2. Carefully butterfly each chicken breast by making a horizontal cut lengthwise, but not cutting all the way through. Open the chicken breasts like a book.
3. Spoon about a quarter of the garlic butter filling onto the center of each opened chicken breast. Fold the chicken breasts back over the garlic butter filling and press the edges to seal.
4. Place the plain flour, beaten eggs, and breadcrumbs in separate shallow dishes. Dip each stuffed chicken breast into the flour, coating it evenly. Shake off any excess flour. Next, dip the floured chicken breast into the beaten eggs, ensuring it is coated thoroughly. Finally, roll the chicken breast in the breadcrumbs, pressing gently to adhere the breadcrumbs to the chicken.
5. In Zone 1 of the air fryer basket, place the coated chicken breasts in a single layer. Select Zone 1 and the AIR FRY program. Set the temperature to 200°C for 20 minutes. Press the START/STOP.
6. After 10 minutes, flip the chicken breasts to ensure even cooking. Continue cooking for the remaining 10 minutes.
7. Let the Chicken Kiev rest for a few minutes before serving. Serve the **Chicken Kiev** hot with your choice of side dishes.

Chapter 03: Poultry

Chicken Nuggets

Prep: **20** Min | Cook: **12** Min | Serves: **4**

Ingredient:

- 500g boneless, skinless chicken breasts
- 60g plain flour
- 2 large eggs, beaten
- 150g breadcrumbs
- 1 teaspoon paprika
- 1/2 teaspoon garlic powder
- 1/2 teaspoon onion powder
- 1/2 teaspoon dried thyme
- 1/2 teaspoon salt
- 1/4 teaspoon black pepper
- Cooking spray or oil, for greasing

Instruction:

1. Cut the chicken breasts into bite-sized pieces, about 2.5cm cubes.
2. In a shallow dish, combine the plain flour, paprika, garlic powder, onion powder, dried thyme, salt, and black pepper.
3. Place the beaten eggs in another shallow dish.
4. In a third shallow dish, spread out the breadcrumbs.
5. Take each piece of chicken and coat it with flour mixture, then dip it into the beaten eggs, and finally coat it with breadcrumbs. Press the breadcrumbs gently to adhere to the chicken. Repeat this process for all the chicken pieces.
6. In Zone 1 of the air fryer basket, place the coated chicken nuggets in a single layer. Avoid overcrowding the basket.
7. Select Zone 1 and the AIR FRY program. Set the temperature to 200°C and the time to 12 minutes. Press the START/STOP button to begin cooking the chicken nuggets.
8. After 6 minutes, open the air fryer and flip the chicken nuggets to ensure even cooking. Close and continue cooking for the remaining 6 minutes.
9. Once the chicken nuggets are golden brown and cooked through, remove them from the air fryer.
10. Serve the **Chicken Nuggets** hot with your choice of dipping sauce and side dishes like fries or a salad.

Chicken Parmesan

Prep: **15** Min | Cook: **25** Min | Serves: **4**

Ingredient:

- 4 chicken breasts (about 600g)
- 100g breadcrumbs
- 50g grated Parmesan cheese
- 2 teaspoons dried Italian seasoning
- 1 teaspoon garlic powder
- 1/2 teaspoon salt
- 1/4 teaspoon black pepper
- 2 large eggs, beaten
- 200g marinara sauce
- 200g shredded mozzarella cheese
- Fresh basil leaves, for garnish

Instruction:

1. In a shallow dish, combine the breadcrumbs, grated Parmesan cheese, dried Italian seasoning, garlic powder, salt, and black pepper.
2. Dip each chicken breast into the beaten eggs, allowing any excess to drip off, and then coat it with the breadcrumb mixture. Press the breadcrumbs gently to adhere to the chicken.
3. In Zone 1 of the air fryer basket, place the coated chicken breasts in a single layer. Avoid overcrowding the basket.
4. Select Zone 1 and the AIR FRY program. Set the temperature to 200°C and the time to 25 minutes. Press the START/STOP.
5. After 12 minutes, open the air fryer and flip the chicken breasts to ensure even cooking. Close and continue cooking for the remaining 13 minutes.
6. Once the chicken is cooked, top each chicken breast with marinara sauce and shredded mozzarella cheese.
7. Select Zone 1 and the AIR FRY program. Set the temperature to 200°C and the time to 5 minutes. Press the START/STOP.
8. After 5 minutes, remove the chicken breasts from the air fryer. Garnish with fresh basil leaves.
9. Serve the **Chicken Parmesan** hot with pasta or a side salad.

Chapter 03: Poultry

Chicken Quesadillas

Prep: **15** Min | Cook: **10** Min | Serves: **2**

Ingredient:

- 2 large flour tortillas (about 25cm in diameter)
- 200g cooked chicken breast, shredded
- 100g grated cheddar cheese
- 50g diced red bell pepper
- 50g diced green bell pepper
- 50g diced onion
- 1 teaspoon olive oil
- 1 teaspoon ground cumin
- 1/2 teaspoon chili powder
- 1/2 teaspoon garlic powder
- Salt and pepper, to taste
- Sour cream and salsa, for serving

Instruction:

1. In a pan, heat the olive oil over medium heat. Add the diced bell peppers and onion, and sauté until they are softened, about 3-4 minutes. Season with ground cumin, chili powder, garlic powder, salt, and pepper. Stir well to combine.
2. In Zone 1 of the air fryer basket, place one flour tortilla. Layer half of the shredded chicken, sautéed vegetables, and grated cheddar cheese on one half of the tortilla. Fold the tortilla in half to create a quesadilla.
3. Grease the air fryer basket with cooking spray or a small amount of oil to prevent sticking.
4. In Zone 1, place one quesadilla in a single layer.
5. Select Zone 1 and the AIR FRY program. Set the temperature to 200°C and the time to 5 minutes. Press the START/STOP button to begin cooking the quesadilla.
6. After 5 minutes, open the air fryer and flip the quesadilla to ensure even cooking. Close and continue cooking for another 5 minutes.
7. Once the quesadilla is golden brown and the cheese is melted, remove it from the air fryer.
8. Let the quesadillas cool for a minute, then cut each quesadilla into wedges. Serve the **Chicken Quesadillas** hot with sour cream and salsa on the side.

Chicken Satay

Prep: **20** Min | Cook: **10** Min | Serves: **4**

Ingredient:

- 400g boneless, skinless chicken breasts
- 3 tablespoons soy sauce
- 2 tablespoons smooth peanut butter
- 2 cloves garlic, minced
- 1 teaspoon curry powder
- 1/2 teaspoon ground cumin
- 1/4 teaspoon chili flakes (adjust to taste)
- Salt, to taste
- Wooden skewers, soaked in water

For the Peanut Sauce:
- 4 tablespoons smooth peanut butter
- 2 tablespoons soy sauce
- 2 tablespoons lime juice
- 1 tablespoon honey
- 2 tsp lime juice
- 2 tsp honey
- 1/4 tsp turmeric
- 1/2 teaspoon chili flakes (adjust to taste)
- Water, as needed

Instruction:

1. In a bowl, combine the soy sauce, peanut butter, lime juice, honey, minced garlic, curry powder, ground cumin, turmeric, chili flakes, and salt. Mix well to make the marinade.
2. Add the chicken strips to the marinade and toss to coat them evenly. Let the chicken marinate for at least 10 minutes.
3. While the chicken is marinating, prepare the peanut sauce. In a separate bowl, combine the peanut butter, soy sauce, lime juice, honey, chili flakes, and a little water to achieve the desired consistency. Mix until smooth. Set aside.
4. Thread the marinated chicken strips onto the soaked woden skewers.
5. Place the chicken skewers in Zone 1. Select Zone 1, choose the AIR FRY program, and set the temperature to 200°C. Set the time to 10 minutes. Press the START/STOP.
6. After 5 minutes of cooking, carefully remove the basket from Zone 1 and flip the skewers. Return the basket to Zone 1 and continue cooking for the remaining 5 minutes.
7. After the cooking time is complete, carefully remove the air fryer basket from Zone 1.
8. Serve the **chicken satay** skewers with the prepared peanut sauce on the side.

Chapter 03: Poultry

Chicken Stir-Fry

Prep: **15** Min | Cook: **15** Min | Serves: **4**

Ingredient:

- 400g boneless, skinless chicken breasts, sliced into strips
- 2 tablespoons soy sauce
- 1 tablespoon oyster sauce
- 1 tablespoon honey
- 1 tablespoon rice vinegar
- 1 teaspoon cornstarch
- 1/2 teaspoon sesame oil
- 1 tablespoon vegetable oil
- 1 red bell pepper, sliced
- 1 yellow bell pepper, sliced
- 1 small onion, sliced
- 100g sugar snap peas, trimmed
- 2 cloves garlic, minced
- 2cm piece of ginger, grated
- Salt and pepper, to taste
- Fresh cilantro, chopped (for garnish)
- Cooked rice or noodles, for serving

Instruction:

1. In a bowl, mix soy sauce, oyster sauce, honey, rice vinegar, cornstarch and sesame oil. Mix well to make sauce. Place the chicken strips in a separate bowl and season with salt and pepper.
2. Pour half of the sauce over the chicken and toss to coat. Reserve the remaining sauce for later.
3. In Zone 1 of the air fryer basket, add the sliced bell peppers, onion, sugar snap peas, minced garlic, and grated ginger. Drizzle the vegetable oil over the vegetables and season with salt and pepper. Toss to coat. In Zone 2, place the marinated chicken strips.
4. Select Zone 1, choose the AIR FRY program, and set the temperature to 200°C. Set the time to 10 minutes. Select MATCH. Press the START/STOP.
5. After 5 minutes of cooking, carefully remove the basket from Zone 1 and shake it to toss the vegetables. Return the basket to Zone 1 and continue cooking for the remaining 5 minutes.
6. After the cooking time is complete, transfer the cooked chicken from Zone 2 into Zone 1 with the vegetables. Pour the remaining sauce over the chicken and vegetables. Toss everything together to coat well. Place back into Zone 1. Select Zone 1 and choose the AIR FRY program, and set the temperature to 200°C. Set the time to 3-5 minutes.
7. After the cooking time is complete, carefully remove the air fryer basket from Zone 1. Serve the **chicken stir-fry** over cooked rice or noodles. Garnish with fresh cilantro.

Chicken Stuffed Peppers

Prep: 15 Min | Cook: 15 Min | Serves: 4

Ingredient:

- 4 large bell peppers (any color)
- 300g cooked chicken breast, shredded
- 100g cooked quinoa
- 1 small onion, diced
- 2 cloves garlic, minced
- 1 teaspoon dried oregano
- 1/2 teaspoon paprika
- 1/2 teaspoon cumin
- Salt and pepper, to taste
- 100g grated cheddar cheese
- Fresh parsley, chopped (for garnish)

Instruction:

1. Slice off the tops of the bell peppers and remove the seeds and membranes. Set aside.
2. In a bowl, combine the shredded chicken, cooked quinoa, diced onion, minced garlic, dried oregano, paprika, cumin, salt, and pepper. Mix well to combine.
3. Stuff each bell pepper with the chicken and quinoa mixture. Pack it tightly, leaving a little space at the top for the cheese.
4. Place the stuffed bell peppers in Zone 1 of the air fryer basket.
5. Select Zone 1, choose the AIR FRY program, and set the temperature to 180°C. Set the time to 15 minutes.
6. Press the START/STOP button to begin cooking.
7. After the cooking time is complete, carefully remove the air fryer basket from Zone 1. The peppers should be tender and slightly charred. Sprinkle the grated cheddar cheese over the top of each stuffed pepper.
8. Place the air fryer basket back into Zone 1. Select Zone 1, choose the AIR FRY program, and set the temperature to 180°C. Set the time to 2 minutes. Press the START/STOP.
9. After the cooking time is complete, carefully remove the air fryer basket from Zone 1. The cheese should be melted and slightly golden. Garnish the **stuffed peppers** with fresh chopped parsley.

Chapter 03: Poultry

Chicken Tenders

Prep: 15 Min | Cook: 15 Min | Serves: 4

Ingredient:

- 500g chicken breast fillets, cut into strips
- 100g all-purpose flour
- 2 teaspoons paprika
- 1 teaspoon garlic powder
- 1 teaspoon onion powder
- 1/2 teaspoon dried thyme
- 1/2 teaspoon dried oregano
- 1/2 teaspoon salt
- 1/4 teaspoon black pepper
- 2 large eggs, beaten
- 100g breadcrumbs
- Cooking spray or oil, for spraying/brushing

Instruction:

1. In a shallow dish, combine the flour, paprika, garlic powder, onion powder, dried thyme, dried oregano, salt, and black pepper. Mix well.
2. In a separate dish, place the beaten eggs.
3. Place the breadcrumbs in another shallow dish.
4. Coat each chicken tender in the flour mixture, shaking off any excess.
5. Dip the floured chicken tender into the beaten eggs, allowing any excess to drip off.
6. Roll the chicken tender in the breadcrumbs, pressing gently to adhere.
7. Place the breaded chicken tenders in Zone 1 of the air fryer basket.
8. Select Zone 1, choose the AIR FRY program, and set the temperature to 200°C. Set the time to 15 minutes.
9. Press the START/STOP button to begin cooking.
10. After 7 minutes of cooking, carefully remove the basket from Zone 1 and flip the chicken tenders. Return the basket to Zone 1 and continue cooking for the remaining 8 minutes.
11. After the cooking time is complete, carefully remove the air fryer basket from Zone 1. The chicken tenders should be golden brown and crispy.
12. Serve the **chicken tenders** with your favorite dipping sauce.

Chicken Teriyaki

Prep: **15** Min | Cook: **15** Min | Serves: **4**

Ingredient:

- 500g boneless, skinless chicken thighs, cut into bite-sized pieces
- 4 tablespoons soy sauce
- 2 tablespoons honey
- 2 tablespoons mirin
- 2 tablespoons rice vinegar
- 1 tablespoon sesame oil
- 2 cloves garlic, minced
- 2cm piece of ginger, grated
- 1 tablespoon cornstarch
- 2 tablespoons water
- Sesame seeds, for garnish
- Sliced green onions, for garnish
- Cooked rice, for serving

Instruction:

1. In a bowl, combine the soy sauce, honey, mirin, rice vinegar, sesame oil, minced garlic, and grated ginger. Mix well to make the teriyaki sauce. Place the chicken pieces in a separate bowl. Pour half of the teriyaki sauce over the chicken and toss to coat. Reserve the remaining sauce for later.
2. In Zone 1, arrange the marinated chicken pieces in a single layer.
3. Select Zone 1, choose the AIR FRY program, and set the temperature to 180°C. Set the time to 15 minutes. Press the START/STOP button to begin cooking.
4. After 10 minutes of cooking, carefully remove the air fryer basket. The chicken should be cooked through and slightly browned.
5. In the meantime, pour the reserved teriyaki sauce into a small saucepan and heat over medium heat.
6. In a separate bowl, mix the cornstarch and water to make a slurry. Add the cornstarch slurry to the saucepan with the teriyaki sauce. Cook, stirring continuously, until the sauce thickens.
7. Place the chicken back into Zone 1. Select Zone 1 and choose the AIR FRY program, and set the temperature to 180°C for to 2 minutes. Press the START/STOP.
8. Serve the **chicken teriyaki** over cooked rice. Garnish with sesame seeds and sliced green onions.

Chapter 03: Poultry

Chicken Wings

Prep: **10** Min | Cook: **25** Min | Serves: **4**

Ingredient:

- 1 kg chicken wings, separated into drumettes and flats
- 2 tablespoons olive oil
- 1 teaspoon paprika
- 1 teaspoon garlic powder
- 1/2 teaspoon salt
- 1/4 teaspoon black pepper
- 100g all-purpose flour
- Cooking spray or oil, for spraying/brushing
- Your choice of dipping sauce (e.g., barbecue sauce, buffalo sauce)

Instruction:

1. In a large bowl, toss the chicken wings with olive oil, paprika, garlic powder, salt, and black pepper. Ensure that the wings are evenly coated with the seasoning.
2. Add the all-purpose flour to the bowl and toss the wings again until they are coated in flour.
3. Evenly dividing chicken wings between the two zones in a single layer. Select Zone 1, choose the AIR FRY program, and set the temperature to 200°C. Set the time to 20 minutes. Select MATCH. Press the START/STOP button to begin cooking.
4. After 10 minutes of cooking, carefully remove both zones. Flip the chicken wings to ensure even cooking.
5. Return both zone and continue cooking for the remaining 10 minutes.
6. After the cooking time is complete, carefully remove both zone. The chicken wings should be golden brown and crispy.
7. If desired, brush or spray the wings with a little cooking oil or cooking spray to enhance their crispiness.
8. Place back into both zone. Select Zone 1, choose the AIR FRY program, and set the temperature to 200°C. Set the time to an additional 5 minutes. Select MATCH. Press the START/STOP.
9. After the additional 5 minutes of cooking time, the wings should be perfectly crispy. Serve the **chicken wings** with your favorite dipping sauce.

Honey Mustard Chicken

Prep: **10** Min | Cook: **20** Min | Serves: **4**

Ingredient:

- 4 boneless, skinless chicken breasts
- 4 tablespoons Dijon mustard
- 2 tablespoons honey
- 1 tablespoon olive oil
- 1 tablespoon lemon juice
- 2 cloves garlic, minced
- 1/2 teaspoon dried thyme
- 1/2 teaspoon salt
- 1/4 teaspoon black pepper
- Cooking spray or oil, for spraying/brushing

...▶ *Instruction:*

1. In a bowl, whisk together the Dijon mustard, honey, olive oil, lemon juice, minced garlic, dried thyme, salt, and black pepper to make the honey mustard marinade.
2. Place the chicken breasts in a shallow dish and pour the honey mustard marinade over them. Ensure that the chicken breasts are well coated on all sides. Let them marinate for 10 minutes.
3. Place the marinated chicken breasts in Zone 1 of the air fryer basket.
4. Select Zone 1, choose the AIR FRY program, and set the temperature to 180°C. Set the time to 20 minutes.
5. Press the START/STOP button to begin cooking.
6. After 10 minutes of cooking, carefully remove the air fryer basket from Zone 1. Flip the chicken breasts to ensure even cooking.
7. Return the basket to Zone 1 and continue cooking for the remaining 10 minutes.
8. After the cooking time is complete, carefully remove the air fryer basket from Zone 1. The chicken breasts should be cooked through and nicely browned.
9. Let the chicken rest for a few minutes before serving.
10. Serve the **honey mustard chicken** with your choice of sides, such as steamed vegetables or a salad.

Chapter 03: Poultry

Lemon Pepper Chicken Wings

Prep: **10** Min | Cook: **25** Min | Serves: **4**

Ingredient:

- 1 kg chicken wings, separated into drumettes and flats
- 2 tablespoons olive oil
- Zest of 1 lemon
- 1 teaspoon ground black pepper
- 1 teaspoon salt
- 1/2 teaspoon garlic powder
- 1/2 teaspoon onion powder
- Cooking spray or oil, for spraying/brushing
- Lemon wedges, for serving

...▶ *Instruction:*

1. In a large bowl, toss the chicken wings with olive oil, lemon zest, ground black pepper, salt, garlic powder, and onion powder. Make sure the wings are evenly coated with the seasoning.
2. Evenly dividing seasoned chicken wings between the two zones in a single layer.
3. Select Zone 1, choose the AIR FRY program, and set the temperature to 200°C. Set the time to 20 minutes. Select MATCH. Press the START/STOP button to begin cooking.
4. After 10 minutes of cooking, carefully remove both zones. Flip the chicken wings to ensure even cooking.
5. Return to both zone and continue cooking for the remaining 10 minutes.
6. After the cooking time is complete. The chicken wings should be golden brown and crispy.
7. If desired, brush or spray the wings with a little cooking oil or cooking spray to enhance their crispiness.
8. Place back into both zones. Select Zone 1, choose the AIR FRY program, and set the temperature to 200°C. Set the time to an additional 5 minutes. Select MATCH. Press the START/STOP button to begin cooking.
9. After the additional 5 minutes of cooking time, the wings should be perfectly crispy and flavorful.
10. Serve the **lemon pepper chicken wings** with lemon wedges on the side.

Lemon Garlic Chicken

Prep: **10** Min | Cook: **20** Min | Serves: **4**

Ingredient:

- 4 boneless, skinless chicken breasts
- 2 tablespoons olive oil
- Zest of 1 lemon
- Juice of 1 lemon
- 4 cloves garlic, minced
- 1 teaspoon dried thyme
- 1/2 teaspoon salt
- 1/4 teaspoon black pepper
- Cooking spray or oil, for spraying/brushing
- Fresh parsley, chopped, for garnish (optional)

Instruction:

1. In a bowl, whisk together the olive oil, lemon zest, lemon juice, minced garlic, dried thyme, salt, and black pepper to make the lemon garlic marinade.
2. Place the chicken breasts in a shallow dish and pour the lemon garlic marinade over them. Ensure that the chicken breasts are well coated on all sides. Let them marinate for 10 minutes.
3. Place the marinated chicken breasts in Zone 1 of the air fryer basket.
4. Select Zone 1, choose the AIR FRY program, and set the temperature to 180°C. Set the time to 20 minutes.
5. Press the START/STOP button to begin cooking.
6. After 10 minutes of cooking, carefully remove the air fryer basket from Zone 1. Flip the chicken breasts to ensure even cooking.
7. Return the basket to Zone 1 and continue cooking for the remaining 10 minutes.
8. After the cooking time is complete, carefully remove the air fryer basket from Zone 1. The chicken breasts should be cooked through and nicely browned.
9. Garnish with fresh parsley, if desired. Serve the **lemon garlic chicken** with your choice of sides, such as roasted vegetables or a salad.

Chapter 03: Poultry

Pesto Chicken Pasta

Prep: **10** Min | Cook: **20** Min | Serves: **4**

Ingredient:

- 300g penne pasta
- 2 boneless, skinless chicken breasts, cut into bite-sized pieces
- 4 tablespoons pesto sauce
- 2 tablespoons olive oil
- 2 cloves garlic, minced
- 1/2 teaspoon salt
- 1/4 teaspoon black pepper
- Grated Parmesan cheese, for serving
- Fresh basil leaves, for garnish (optional)

Instruction:

1. Cook the penne pasta according to the package instructions until al dente. Drain and set aside.
2. In a bowl, combine the chicken pieces, pesto sauce, olive oil, minced garlic, salt, and black pepper. Toss until the chicken is well coated with the pesto mixture.
3. Place the pesto-coated chicken pieces in Zone 1 of the air fryer basket.
4. Select Zone 1, choose the AIR FRY program, and set the temperature to 180°C. Set the time to 15 minutes.
5. Press the START/STOP button to begin cooking.
6. After 7 minutes of cooking, carefully remove the air fryer basket from Zone 1. Flip the chicken pieces to ensure even cooking.
7. Return the basket to Zone 1 and continue cooking for the remaining 8 minutes.
8. After the cooking time is complete, carefully remove the air fryer basket from Zone 1. The chicken should be cooked through and slightly browned.
9. In a large serving bowl, combine the cooked penne pasta and the cooked pesto chicken.
10. Toss the pasta and chicken together until well mixed.
11. Serve the **pesto chicken pasta** with grated Parmesan cheese on top and garnish with fresh basil leaves, if desired.

Roast Chicken Pieces

Prep: **10** Min | Cook: **30** Min | Serves: **4**

Ingredient:

- 1 kg chicken pieces (such as drumsticks and thighs)
- 2 tablespoons olive oil
- 1 teaspoon dried thyme
- 1 teaspoon dried rosemary
- 1 teaspoon garlic powder
- 1/2 teaspoon onion powder
- 1/2 teaspoon paprika
- 1/2 teaspoon salt
- 1/4 teaspoon black pepper
- Cooking spray or oil, for spraying/brushing

Instruction:

1. In a small bowl, combine the dried thyme, dried rosemary, garlic powder, onion powder, paprika, salt, and black pepper to make the seasoning mixture.
2. Pat the chicken pieces dry with paper towels.
3. Brush or rub the chicken pieces with olive oil to coat them evenly.
4. Sprinkle the seasoning mixture over the chicken pieces, making sure to cover them on all sides.
5. Evenly dividing seasoned chicken pieces between the two zones.
6. Select Zone 1, choose the ROAST program, and set the temperature to 200°C. Set the time to 30 minutes. Select MATCH. Press the START/STOP button to begin cooking.
7. After 15 minutes of cooking, flip the chicken pieces to ensure even cooking and continue cooking for the remaining 15 minutes.
8. After the cooking time is complete, carefully remove the air fryer basket from both zone. The chicken pieces should be cooked through, golden brown, and crispy.
9. Let the chicken rest for a few minutes before serving.
10. Serve the **roast chicken pieces** with your choice of sides, such as roasted potatoes and vegetables.

Chapter 03: Poultry

Tandoori Chicken

Prep: **15** Min | Cook: **25** Min | Serves: **4**

Ingredient:

- 800g bone-in chicken pieces (such as drumsticks and thighs)
- 200g plain yogurt
- 3 tablespoons lemon juice
- 2 tablespoons vegetable oil
- 4 cloves garlic, minced
- 2 teaspoons ground cumin
- 2 teaspoons ground coriander
- 2 teaspoons paprika
- 2 teaspoons ground turmeric
- 1 teaspoon ground ginger
- 1 teaspoon salt
- 1/2 teaspoon cayenne pepper (adjust to taste)
- Fresh cilantro leaves, for garnish (optional)
- Lemon wedges, for serving (optional)

Instruction:

1. In a bowl, combine the yogurt, lemon juice, vegetable oil, minced garlic, ground cumin, ground coriander, paprika, ground turmeric, ground ginger, salt, and cayenne pepper to make the marinade.
2. Place the chicken pieces in a shallow dish and pour the marinade over them. Ensure that the chicken pieces are well coated on all sides. Let them marinate for at least 1 hour, or preferably overnight in the refrigerator.
3. Evenly dividing marinated chicken pieces between the two zone.
4. Select Zone 1, choose the AIR FRY program, and set the temperature to 200°C. Set the time to 25 minutes. Select MATCH. Press the START/STOP button to begin cooking.
5. After 15 minutes of cooking, flip the chicken pieces to ensure even cooking and continue cooking for the remaining 10 minutes.
6. After the cooking time is complete, the chicken pieces should be cooked through with a nicely charred and flavorful exterior.
7. Let the chicken rest for a few minutes.
8. Garnish with fresh cilantro leaves, if desired, and serve with lemon wedges on the side.
9. Enjoy your delicious **Tandoori Chicken**!

Baked Cod with Herbs

Prep: **10** Min | Cook: **12** Min | Serves: **4**

Ingredient:

- 4 cod fillets (about 150g each)
- 2 tablespoons olive oil
- 1 tablespoon fresh lemon juice
- 2 cloves garlic, minced
- 1 tablespoon chopped fresh parsley
- 1 teaspoon chopped fresh thyme
- 1 teaspoon chopped fresh dill
- 1/2 teaspoon salt
- 1/4 teaspoon black pepper
- Lemon wedges, for serving (optional)

Instruction:

1. In a small bowl, combine the olive oil, lemon juice, minced garlic, chopped parsley, chopped thyme, chopped dill, salt, and black pepper to make the herb mixture.
2. Place the cod fillets on a plate and brush both sides with the herb mixture. Ensure that the fillets are well coated.
3. Place the coated cod fillets in Zone 1 of the air fryer basket.
4. Select Zone 1, choose the AIR FRY program, and set the temperature to 200°C. Set the time to 12 minutes.
5. Press the START/STOP button to begin cooking.
6. After 6 minutes of cooking, carefully remove the air fryer basket from Zone 1. Flip the cod fillets to ensure even cooking.
7. Return the basket to Zone 1 and continue cooking for the remaining 6 minutes.
8. After the cooking time is complete, carefully remove the air fryer basket from Zone 1. The cod fillets should be opaque and flake easily with a fork.
9. Serve the baked cod fillets with lemon wedges on the side, if desired.
10. Enjoy your delicious **Baked Cod with Herbs**!

Chapter 04: Fish & Seafood

Baked Sea Bass with Lemon and Dill

Prep: **10** Min | Cook: **10** Min | Serves: **4**

Ingredient:

- 4 sea bass fillets (about 150g each)
- 2 tablespoons olive oil
- 2 tablespoons fresh lemon juice
- Zest of 1 lemon
- 2 cloves garlic, minced
- 1 tablespoon chopped fresh dill
- 1/2 teaspoon salt
- 1/4 teaspoon black pepper
- Lemon wedges, for serving (optional)

Instruction:

1. In a small bowl, combine the olive oil, lemon juice, lemon zest, minced garlic, chopped dill, salt, and black pepper to make the marinade.
2. Place the sea bass fillets on a plate and brush both sides with the marinade. Ensure that the fillets are well coated.
3. Place the coated sea bass fillets in Zone 1 of the air fryer basket.
4. Select Zone 1, choose the AIR FRY program, and set the temperature to 200°C. Set the time to 10 minutes.
5. Press the START/STOP button to begin cooking.
6. After 5 minutes of cooking, carefully remove the air fryer basket from Zone 1. Flip the sea bass fillets to ensure even cooking.
7. Return the basket to Zone 1 and continue cooking for the remaining 5 minutes.
8. After the cooking time is complete, carefully remove the air fryer basket from Zone 1. The sea bass fillets should be opaque and flake easily with a fork.
9. Serve the baked sea bass fillets with lemon wedges on the side, if desired.
10. Enjoy your delicious **Baked Sea Bass with Lemon and Dill**!

Blackened Cajun Tilapia

Prep: **10** Min | Cook: **12** Min | Serves: **4**

Ingredient:

- 4 tilapia fillets (about 150g each)
- 2 tablespoons olive oil
- 2 teaspoons Cajun seasoning
- 1 teaspoon paprika
- 1/2 teaspoon dried thyme
- 1/2 teaspoon dried oregano
- 1/2 teaspoon garlic powder
- 1/2 teaspoon onion powder
- 1/2 teaspoon salt
- 1/4 teaspoon black pepper
- Lemon wedges, for serving (optional)

Instruction:

1. In a small bowl, combine the Cajun seasoning, paprika, dried thyme, dried oregano, garlic powder, onion powder, salt, and black pepper to make the spice rub.
2. Brush both sides of the tilapia fillets with olive oil.
3. Sprinkle the spice rub evenly over both sides of the tilapia fillets, pressing it gently to adhere.
4. Place the seasoned tilapia fillets in Zone 1 of the air fryer basket.
5. Select Zone 1, choose the AIR FRY program, and set the temperature to 200°C. Set the time to 12 minutes.
6. Press the START/STOP button to begin cooking.
7. After 6 minutes of cooking, carefully remove the air fryer basket from Zone 1. Flip the tilapia fillets to ensure even cooking.
8. Return the basket to Zone 1 and continue cooking for the remaining 6 minutes.
9. After the cooking time is complete, carefully remove the air fryer basket from Zone 1. The tilapia fillets should be opaque and flake easily with a fork.
10. Serve the **blackened Cajun tilapia** fillets with lemon wedges on the side, if desired.

Chapter 04: Fish & Seafood

Cajun Salmon Fillets

Prep: **10** Min | Cook: **10** Min | Serves: **4**

Ingredient:

- 4 salmon fillets (about 150g each)
- 2 tablespoons olive oil
- 2 teaspoons Cajun seasoning
- 1 teaspoon paprika
- 1/2 teaspoon dried thyme
- 1/2 teaspoon dried oregano
- 1/2 teaspoon garlic powder
- 1/2 teaspoon onion powder
- 1/2 teaspoon salt
- 1/4 teaspoon black pepper
- Lemon wedges, for serving (optional)

Instruction:

1. In a small bowl, combine the Cajun seasoning, paprika, dried thyme, dried oregano, garlic powder, onion powder, salt, and black pepper to make the spice rub.
2. Brush both sides of the salmon fillets with olive oil.
3. Sprinkle the spice rub evenly over both sides of the salmon fillets, pressing it gently to adhere.
4. Place the seasoned salmon fillets in Zone 1 of the air fryer basket.
5. Select Zone 1, choose the AIR FRY program, and set the temperature to 200°C. Set the time to 10 minutes.
6. Press the START/STOP button to begin cooking.
7. After 5 minutes of cooking, carefully remove the air fryer basket from Zone 1. Flip the salmon fillets to ensure even cooking.
8. Return the basket to Zone 1 and continue cooking for the remaining 5 minutes.
9. After the cooking time is complete, carefully remove the air fryer basket from Zone 1. The salmon fillets should be opaque and flake easily with a fork.
10. Serve the **Cajun salmon fillets** with lemon wedges on the side, if desired.

Coconut Curry Shrimp

Prep: **10** Min | Cook: **15** Min | Serves: **4**

Ingredient:

- 500g shrimp, peeled and deveined
- 2 tablespoons olive oil
- 1 red bell pepper, diced
- 2 tablespoons curry powder
- 1 teaspoon ground cumin
- 1 teaspoon ground coriander
- 1/2 teaspoon turmeric
- 1/2 teaspoon chili powder (adjust to taste)
- 400ml can coconut milk
- 1 tablespoon tomato paste
- 1 tablespoon fish sauce (optional)
- 1 tablespoon lime juice
- Fresh cilantro, for garnish
- Cooked rice, for serving
- 1 onion, finely chopped
- 2 cloves garlic, minced
- Salt, to taste

Instruction:

1. In a large bowl, combine the shrimp, curry powder, ground cumin, ground coriander, turmeric, and chili powder. Toss well to coat the shrimp with the spices.
2. In Zone 1, add the onion, garlic, and red bell pepper. Drizzle with olive oil and toss to coat. Select Zone 1, choose the AIR FRY program, and set the temperature to 200°C. Set the time to 15 minutes. Press the START/STOP.
3. After 5 minutes, carefully remove the air fryer basket from Zone 1. Add the seasoned shrimp to Zone 1 with the onion, garlic, and red bell pepper. Return the basket to Zone 1 and continue cooking for another 5 minutes.
4. In the meantime, in a medium-sized saucepan, add the coconut milk, tomato paste, fish sauce (if using), lime juice, and salt. Heat over medium heat, stirring occasionally, until the sauce is heated through.
5. Once the shrimp is cooked, .pour the coconut curry sauce over the shrimp and vegetables in Zone 1. Stir well to coat everything in the sauce. Return the basket to Zone 1 and continue cooking for the remaining 5 minutes.
6. Serve the **Coconut Curry Shrimp** over cooked rice. Garnish with fresh cilantro.

Chapter 04: Fish & Seafood

Coconut Crusted Fish

Prep: **15** Min | Cook: **12** Min | Serves: **4**

Ingredient:

- 4 white fish fillets (such as cod or haddock), about 150g each
- 60g all-purpose flour
- 2 large eggs, beaten
- 80g desiccated coconut
- 1/2 teaspoon salt
- 1/4 teaspoon black pepper
- Lemon wedges, for serving (optional)
- Tartar sauce, for serving (optional)

Instruction:

1. Place the flour in a shallow dish or plate.
2. In another shallow dish or plate, combine the beaten eggs.
3. In a third shallow dish or plate, mix together the desiccated coconut, salt, and black pepper.
4. Dip each fish fillet into the flour, coating it evenly on both sides. Shake off any excess flour.
5. Dip the floured fish fillet into the beaten eggs, allowing any excess to drip off.
6. Press the fish fillet into the coconut mixture, ensuring it is completely coated with coconut on all sides.
7. Place the coated fish fillets in Zone 1 . Select Zone 1, choose the AIR FRY program, and set the temperature to 200°C. Set the time to 12 minutes. Press the START/STOP button to begin cooking.
8. After 6 minutes of cooking, carefully remove the air fryer basket from Zone 1. Flip the fish fillets to ensure even cooking and browning.
9. Return the basket to Zone 1 and continue cooking for the remaining 6 minutes.
10. After the cooking time is complete, carefully remove the air fryer basket from Zone 1. The coconut-crusted fish fillets should be golden brown and crispy.
11. Serve the **Coconut Crusted Fish** with lemon wedges and tartar sauce on the side, if desired.

Cod Fillets

Prep: **10** Min | Cook: **12** Min | Serves: **4**

Ingredient:

- 4 cod fillets, about 150g each
- 2 tablespoons olive oil
- 1 teaspoon dried parsley
- 1/2 teaspoon garlic powder
- 1/2 teaspoon paprika
- 1/2 teaspoon salt
- 1/4 teaspoon black pepper
- Lemon wedges, for serving (optional)
- Tartar sauce, for serving (optional)

Instruction:

1. In a small bowl, combine the dried parsley, garlic powder, paprika, salt, and black pepper to make the seasoning mixture.
2. Brush both sides of the cod fillets with olive oil.
3. Sprinkle the seasoning mixture evenly over both sides of the cod fillets, pressing it gently to adhere.
4. Place the seasoned cod fillets in Zone 1 of the air fryer basket.
5. Select Zone 1, choose the AIR FRY program, and set the temperature to 200°C. Set the time to 12 minutes.
6. Press the START/STOP button to begin cooking.
7. After 6 minutes of cooking, carefully remove the air fryer basket from Zone 1. Flip the cod fillets to ensure even cooking and browning.
8. Return the basket to Zone 1 and continue cooking for the remaining 6 minutes.
9. After the cooking time is complete, carefully remove the air fryer basket from Zone 1. The cod fillets should be opaque and flake easily with a fork.
10. Serve the **Cod Fillets** with lemon wedges and tartar sauce on the side, if desired.

Chapter 04: Fish & Seafood

Fish Burger Patties

Prep: **15** Min | Cook: **10** Min | Serves: **4**

Ingredient:

- 500g white fish fillets (such as cod or haddock), skinless and boneless
- 25g breadcrumbs
- 15g finely chopped fresh parsley
- 30g finely chopped red onion
- 1 tablespoon lemon juice
- 1 teaspoon Dijon mustard
- 1/2 teaspoon salt
- 1/4 teaspoon black pepper
- 4 burger buns
- Lettuce leaves, tomato slices, and condiments of your choice, for serving

Instruction:

1. In a food processor, pulse the white fish fillets until they are finely chopped but not pureed.
2. In a large bowl, combine the chopped fish, breadcrumbs, parsley, red onion, lemon juice, Dijon mustard, salt, and black pepper. Mix well to combine all the ingredients.
3. Divide the mixture into 4 equal portions. Shape each portion into a patty about 2cm thick.
4. Place the fish burger patties in Zone 1 of the air fryer basket.
5. Select Zone 1, choose the AIR FRY program, and set the temperature to 200°C. Set the time to 10 minutes.
6. Press the START/STOP button to begin cooking.
7. After 5 minutes of cooking, carefully remove the air fryer basket from Zone 1. Flip the fish burger patties to ensure even cooking and browning.
8. Return the basket to Zone 1 and continue cooking for the remaining 5 minutes.
9. After the cooking time is complete, carefully remove the air fryer basket from Zone 1. The fish burger patties should be golden brown and cooked through.
10. Assemble the burger by placing a fish patty on the bottom half of each burger bun. Top with lettuce leaves, tomato slices, and any condiments of your choice. Place the top half of the bun on top.
11. Serve the **Fish Burger Patties** immediately.

Fish Tandoori Skewers

Prep: **20** Min | Cook: **10** Min | Serves: **4**

Ingredient:

- 500g white fish fillets (such as cod or haddock), cut into 2cm cubes
- 200g Greek yogurt
- 2 tablespoons lemon juice
- 2 tablespoons tandoori masala paste
- 1 tablespoon vegetable oil
- 2 cloves garlic, minced
- 1 teaspoon ground cumin
- 1 teaspoon ground coriander
- 1/2 teaspoon turmeric
- 1/2 teaspoon salt
- 1/4 teaspoon cayenne pepper (optional for spice)
- Fresh coriander leaves, for garnish
- Lemon wedges, for serving (optional)

Instruction:

1. In a large bowl, combine the Greek yogurt, lemon juice, tandoori masala paste, vegetable oil, minced garlic, ground cumin, ground coriander, turmeric, salt, and cayenne pepper (if using). Mix well to form a marinade.
2. Add the fish cubes to the marinade, ensuring they are well coated. Allow the fish to marinate for at least 15 minutes.
3. Thread the marinated fish cubes onto skewers, leaving a small gap between each piece.
4. Place the fish skewers in Zone 1 of the air fryer basket.
5. Select Zone 1, choose the AIR FRY program, and set the temperature to 200°C. Set the time to 10 minutes.
6. Press the START/STOP button to begin cooking.
7. After 5 minutes of cooking, carefully remove the air fryer basket from Zone 1. Flip the fish skewers to ensure even cooking.
8. Return the basket to Zone 1 and continue cooking for the remaining 5 minutes.
9. After the cooking time is complete, carefully remove the air fryer basket from Zone 1. The fish should be cooked through and slightly charred.
10. Garnish the **Fish Tandoori Skewers** with fresh coriander leaves.
11. Serve the skewers with lemon wedges on the side, if desired.

Chapter 04: Fish & Seafood

Garlic Parmesan Crusted Salmon

Prep: **10** Min | Cook: **10** Min | Serves: **4**

Ingredient:

- 4 salmon fillets, about 150g each
- 2 tablespoons melted butter
- 2 cloves garlic, minced
- 25g grated Parmesan cheese
- 2 tablespoons breadcrumbs
- 1 tablespoon chopped fresh parsley
- 1/2 teaspoon salt
- 1/4 teaspoon black pepper
- Lemon wedges, for serving (optional)

Instruction:

1. In a small bowl, combine the melted butter and minced garlic.
2. In another bowl, mix together the grated Parmesan cheese, breadcrumbs, chopped parsley, salt, and black pepper.
3. Brush both sides of each salmon fillet with the garlic butter mixture.
4. Dip each fillet into the Parmesan breadcrumb mixture, pressing gently to adhere and coat the salmon evenly.
5. Place the coated salmon fillets in Zone 1 of the air fryer basket.
6. Select Zone 1, choose the AIR FRY program, and set the temperature to 200°C. Set the time to 10 minutes.
7. Press the START/STOP button to begin cooking.
8. After 5 minutes of cooking, carefully remove the air fryer basket from Zone 1. Flip the salmon fillets to ensure even cooking and browning.
9. Return the basket to Zone 1 and continue cooking for the remaining 5 minutes.
10. After the cooking time is complete, carefully remove the air fryer basket from Zone 1. The salmon should be cooked through and the crust should be golden brown.
11. Serve the **Garlic Parmesan Crusted Salmon** with lemon wedges on the side, if desired.

Grilled Halibut Steaks

Prep: **10** Min | Cook: **10** Min | Serves: **4**

Ingredient:

- 4 halibut steaks, about 200g each
- 2 tablespoons olive oil
- 2 tablespoons lemon juice
- 2 cloves garlic, minced
- 1 teaspoon dried thyme
- 1/2 teaspoon salt
- 1/4 teaspoon black pepper
- Lemon wedges, for serving (optional)

Instruction:

1. In a small bowl, whisk together the olive oil, lemon juice, minced garlic, dried thyme, salt, and black pepper.
2. Place the halibut steaks in a shallow dish and pour the marinade over them. Allow the steaks to marinate for about 10 minutes, turning them once halfway through.
3. Remove the halibut steaks from the marinade, allowing any excess marinade to drip off.
4. Evenly dividing halibut steaks between the two zone.
5. Select Zone 1, choose the AIR FRY program, and set the temperature to 200°C. Set the time to 10 minutes. Select MATCH. Press the START/STOP button to begin cooking.
6. After 5 minutes of cooking, flip the halibut steaks to ensure even cooking and continue cooking for the remaining 5 minutes.
7. After the cooking time is complete, carefully remove the air fryer basket from both zone. The halibut steaks should be cooked through and flaky.
8. Serve the **Grilled Halibut Steaks** with lemon wedges on the side, if desired.

Chapter 04: Fish & Seafood

Grilled Lobster Tails

Prep: **15** Min | Cook: **12** Min | Serves: **4**

Ingredient:

- 4 lobster tails
- 4 tablespoons melted butter
- 2 cloves garlic, minced
- 1 tablespoon chopped fresh parsley
- 1/2 teaspoon salt
- 1/4 teaspoon black pepper
- Lemon wedges, for serving (optional)

Instruction:

1. Using kitchen shears, carefully cut the top shell of each lobster tail lengthwise, starting from the open end and cutting towards the tail, but not through the tail.
2. Gently lift the meat of each lobster tail and place it on top of the shell, keeping it attached near the tail.
3. In a small bowl, combine the melted butter, minced garlic, chopped parsley, salt, and black pepper.
4. Brush the butter mixture over the exposed meat of each lobster tail, ensuring it's evenly coated.
5. Place the lobster tails in Zone 1 of the air fryer basket, with the meat side facing up.
6. Select Zone 1, choose the AIR FRY program, and set the temperature to 200°C. Set the time to 8 minutes.
7. Press the START/STOP button to begin cooking.
8. After 4 minutes of cooking, carefully remove the air fryer basket from Zone 1. Brush the lobster tails with the remaining butter mixture.
9. Return the basket to Zone 1 and continue cooking for the remaining 4 minutes, or until the lobster meat is opaque and cooked through.
10. Carefully remove the lobster tails from the air fryer basket and let them rest for a minute before serving.
11. Serve the **Grilled Lobster Tails** with lemon wedges on the side, if desired.

Grilled Mackerel

Prep: **10** Min | Cook: **10** Min | Serves: **4**

Ingredient:

- 4 mackerel fillets
- 2 tablespoons olive oil
- 2 tablespoons lemon juice
- 2 cloves garlic, minced
- 1 teaspoon dried thyme
- 1/2 teaspoon salt
- 1/4 teaspoon black pepper
- Lemon wedges, for serving (optional)

...▶ *Instruction:*

1. In a small bowl, whisk together the olive oil, lemon juice, minced garlic, dried thyme, salt, and black pepper.
2. Place the mackerel fillets in a shallow dish and pour the marinade over them. Allow the fillets to marinate for about 10 minutes, turning them once halfway through.
3. Remove the mackerel fillets from the marinade, allowing any excess marinade to drip off.
4. Evenly dividing fillets between the two zone.
5. Select Zone 1, choose the AIR FRY program, and set the temperature to 200°C. Set the time to 10 minutes. Select MATCH. Press the START/STOP button to begin cooking.
6. After 5 minutes of cooking, flip the mackerel fillets to ensure even cooking and continue cooking for the remaining 5 minutes.
7. After the cooking time is complete, carefully remove the air fryer basket from both zone. The mackerel fillets should be cooked through and flaky.
8. Serve the **Grilled Mackerel** with lemon wedges on the side, if desired.

Chapter 04: Fish & Seafood

Haddock Fillets

Prep: **10** Min | Cook: **12** Min | Serves: **4**

Ingredient:

- 4 haddock fillets, about 150g each
- 2 tablespoons olive oil
- 1 tablespoon lemon juice
- 1 teaspoon paprika
- 1/2 teaspoon garlic powder
- 1/2 teaspoon dried thyme
- 1/2 teaspoon salt
- 1/4 teaspoon black pepper
- Lemon wedges, for serving (optional)

...▶ *Instruction:*

1. In a small bowl, whisk together the olive oil, lemon juice, paprika, garlic powder, dried thyme, salt, and black pepper.
2. Place the haddock fillets in a shallow dish and pour the marinade over them. Allow the fillets to marinate for about 10 minutes, turning them once halfway through.
3. Remove the haddock fillets from the marinade, allowing any excess marinade to drip off.
4. Evenly dividing fillets between the two zone.
5. Select Zone 1, choose the AIR FRY program, and set the temperature to 200°C. Set the time to 12 minutes. Select MATCH to duplicate settings across both zones. Press the START/STOP button to begin cooking.
6. After 6 minutes of cooking, flip the haddock fillets to ensure even cooking and continue cooking for the remaining 6 minutes.
7. After the cooking time is complete, carefully remove the air fryer basket from both zone. The haddock fillets should be cooked through and flaky.
8. Serve the **Haddock Fillets** with lemon wedges on the side, if desired.

Lemon Garlic Butter Cod

Prep: **10** Min | Cook: **10** Min | Serves: **4**

Ingredient:

- 4 cod fillets, about 150g each
- 4 tablespoons unsalted butter, melted
- 2 cloves garlic, minced
- 2 tablespoons lemon juice
- 1 teaspoon lemon zest
- 1 tablespoon chopped fresh parsley
- 1/2 teaspoon salt
- 1/4 teaspoon black pepper
- Lemon wedges, for serving (optional)

...▶ *Instruction:*

1. In a small bowl, combine the melted butter, minced garlic, lemon juice, lemon zest, chopped parsley, salt, and black pepper.
2. Place the cod fillets in a shallow dish and pour the lemon garlic butter mixture over them. Make sure the fillets are evenly coated. Let them marinate for about 10 minutes.
3. Remove the cod fillets from the marinade, allowing any excess marinade to drip off.
4. Place the fillets in Zone 1 of the air fryer basket.
5. Select Zone 1, choose the AIR FRY program, and set the temperature to 200°C. Set the time to 10 minutes.
6. Press the START/STOP button to begin cooking.
7. After 5 minutes of cooking, carefully remove the air fryer basket from Zone 1. Brush the cod fillets with any remaining marinade.
8. Return the basket to Zone 1 and continue cooking for the remaining 5 minutes.
9. After the cooking time is complete, carefully remove the air fryer basket from Zone 1. The cod fillets should be cooked through and flaky.
10. Serve the **Lemon Garlic Butter Cod** with lemon wedges on the side, if desired.

Chapter 04: Fish & Seafood

Mustard-Crusted Salmon

Prep: **10** Min | Cook: **12** Min | Serves: **4**

Ingredient:

- 4 salmon fillets, about 150g each
- 4 tablespoons Dijon mustard
- 2 tablespoons honey
- 1 tablespoon lemon juice
- 1 teaspoon lemon zest
- 1/2 teaspoon dried dill
- 1/2 teaspoon salt
- 1/4 teaspoon black pepper
- Lemon wedges, for serving (optional)

...▶ *Instruction:*

1. In a small bowl, whisk together the Dijon mustard, honey, lemon juice, lemon zest, dried dill, salt, and black pepper.
2. Place the salmon fillets on a plate or a shallow dish. Spread the mustard mixture evenly over the top of each fillet, coating them well. Let them marinate for about 10 minutes.
3. Place the fillets in Zone 1 of the air fryer basket.
4. Select Zone 1, choose the AIR FRY program, and set the temperature to 200°C. Set the time to 12 minutes.
5. Press the START/STOP button to begin cooking.
6. After 6 minutes of cooking, carefully remove the air fryer basket from Zone 1. The mustard crust should be starting to brown.
7. Return the basket to Zone 1 and continue cooking for the remaining 6 minutes, or until the salmon is cooked through and flakes easily with a fork.
8. After the cooking time is complete, carefully remove the air fryer basket from Zone 1. The Mustard-Crusted Salmon should be cooked to perfection.
9. Serve the salmon fillets with lemon wedges on the side, if desired.
10. Enjoy your delicious **Mustard-Crusted Salmon**!

Plaice Fillets

Prep: **10** Min | Cook: **8** Min | Serves: **4**

Ingredient:

- 4 plaice fillets, about 150g each
- 2 tablespoons plain flour
- 1 teaspoon paprika
- 1/2 teaspoon salt
- 1/4 teaspoon black pepper
- 2 tablespoons vegetable oil
- Lemon wedges, for serving (optional)

...▶ *Instruction:*

1. In a shallow dish, combine the plain flour, paprika, salt, and black pepper.
2. Dredge each plaice fillet in the flour mixture, shaking off any excess.
3. Evenly dividing fillets between the two zones, ensuring they are in a single layer.
4. Select Zone 1, choose the AIR FRY program, and set the temperature to 200°C. Set the time to 8 minutes. Select MATCH to duplicate settings across both zones. Press the START/STOP button to begin cooking.
5. After 4 minutes of cooking, drizzle the vegetable oil over the fillets to help them crisp up and continue cooking for the remaining 4 minutes.
6. After the cooking time is complete, carefully remove the air fryer basket from both zone. The Plaice Fillets should be crispy and golden brown.
7. Serve the plaice fillets with lemon wedges on the side, if desired.
8. Enjoy your delicious **Plaice Fillets**!

Chapter 04: Fish & Seafood

Pesto Grilled Swordfish

Prep: **10** Min | Cook: **10** Min | Serves: **4**

Ingredient:

- 4 swordfish steaks, about 150g each
- 4 tablespoons pesto sauce
- 1 tablespoon lemon juice
- 1/2 teaspoon salt
- 1/4 teaspoon black pepper
- Lemon wedges, for serving (optional)

...▶ *Instruction:*

1. In a small bowl, combine the pesto sauce, lemon juice, salt, and black pepper.
2. Place the swordfish steaks in a shallow dish and spoon the pesto mixture over them. Make sure the steaks are evenly coated. Let them marinate for about 10 minutes.
3. Remove the swordfish steaks from the marinade, allowing any excess marinade to drip off.
4. Evenly dividing steaks between the two zones, ensuring they are in a single layer.
5. Select Zone 1, choose the AIR FRY program, and set the temperature to 200°C. Set the time to 10 minutes. Select MATCH to duplicate settings across both zones. Press the START/STOP button to begin cooking.
6. After 5 minutes of cooking, brush any remaining marinade over the swordfish steaks and continue cooking for the remaining 5 minutes.
7. After the cooking time is complete, carefully remove the air fryer basket from both zone. The swordfish steaks should be cooked through and lightly browned.
8. Serve the **Pesto Grilled Swordfish** with lemon wedges on the side, if desired.

Shrimp and Crab Linguine

Prep: **10** Min | Cook: **15** Min | Serves: **2**

Ingredient:

- 200g linguine pasta
- 200g shrimp, peeled and deveined
- 150g crab meat, drained and flaked
- 2 tablespoons olive oil
- 2 cloves garlic, minced
- 1 small onion, finely chopped
- 1 red chili, finely chopped (optional)
- 200ml double cream
- 50g grated Parmesan cheese
- 2 tablespoons chopped fresh parsley
- Salt and pepper to taste

...▶ Instruction:

1. Cook the linguine pasta according to the package instructions until al dente. Drain and set aside.
2. In Zone 1 of the air fryer, add the shrimp, olive oil, minced garlic, chopped onion, and red chili. Select Zone 1, choose the AIR FRY program, and set the time to 4-5 minutes at 180°C. Press START/STOP.
3. After 2-3 minutes of air frying, open the lid of Zone 1 and carefully flip the shrimp using tongs or a spatula for even cooking.
4. Close the lid and continue air frying for another 2-3 minutes until the shrimp are cooked through and pink.
5. Remove the cooked shrimp from Zone 1 of the air fryer and set them aside.
6. In Zone 2 of the air fryer, add the double cream, grated Parmesan cheese, chopped parsley, salt, and pepper. Select Zone 2, choose the AIR FRY program, and set the time to 3-4 minutes at 180°C. Press START/STOP.
7. After 2 minutes of air frying, open the lid of Zone 2 and add the cooked linguine pasta, flaked crab meat, and cooked shrimp. Close the lid and continue air frying for another 1-2 minutes.
8. Serve **Shrimp and Crab Linguine** hot with lemon wedges on the side.

Chapter 04: Fish & Seafood

Sea Bass Fillets

Prep: **10** Min | Cook: **12** Min | Serves: **4**

Ingredient:

- 4 sea bass fillets, about 150g each
- 2 tablespoons olive oil
- 1 teaspoon dried thyme
- 1 teaspoon garlic powder
- 1/2 teaspoon salt
- 1/4 teaspoon black pepper
- Lemon wedges, for serving (optional)

...▶ Instruction:

1. In a small bowl, combine the olive oil, dried thyme, garlic powder, salt, and black pepper. Mix well to make a seasoning mixture.
2. Pat the sea bass fillets dry with a paper towel. Place them on a plate or cutting board.
3. Rub the seasoning mixture evenly over both sides of the sea bass fillets.
4. Place the fillets in Zone 1 of the air fryer basket.
5. Select Zone 1, choose the AIR FRY program, and set the temperature to 200°C. Set the time to 12 minutes.
6. Press the START/STOP button to begin cooking.
7. After 6 minutes of cooking, carefully remove the air fryer basket from Zone 1. Flip the sea bass fillets over using tongs or a spatula.
8. Return the basket to Zone 1 and continue cooking for the remaining 6 minutes, or until the sea bass is cooked through and flakes easily with a fork.
9. After the cooking time is complete, carefully remove the air fryer basket from Zone 1. The sea bass fillets should be cooked to perfection, with a crispy exterior and tender interior.
10. Serve the **Sea Bass Fillets** with lemon wedges on the side, if desired.

Shrimp and Vegetable Stir-Fry

Prep: **15** Min | Cook: **2** Min | Serves: **4**

Ingredient:

- 300g shrimp, peeled and deveined
- 1 red bell pepper, sliced
- 1 yellow bell pepper, sliced
- 1 small courgette (zucchini), sliced
- 1 small carrot, julienned
- 100g sugar snap peas
- 2 cloves garlic, minced
- 2 tablespoons soy sauce
- 1 tablespoon oyster sauce
- 1 tablespoon cornstarch
- 1 teaspoon sesame oil
- 1 tablespoon vegetable oil
- Salt and pepper, to taste
- Fresh coriander, chopped, for garnish

Instruction:

1. In a small bowl, whisk together the soy sauce, oyster sauce, cornstarch, and sesame oil to make a sauce. Set aside.
2. In Zone 1 of the air fryer basket, place the shrimp, red bell pepper, yellow bell pepper, courgette, carrot, and sugar snap peas.
3. Drizzle the vegetable oil over the shrimp and vegetables. Season with salt and pepper to taste. Toss to coat evenly.
4. Select Zone 1, choose the AIR FRY program, and set the temperature to 200°C. Set the time to 12 minutes.
5. Press the START/STOP button to begin cooking.
6. After 6 minutes of cooking, carefully remove the air fryer basket from Zone 1. Add the minced garlic and pour the sauce over the shrimp and vegetables.
7. Return the basket to Zone 1 and continue cooking for the remaining 6 minutes, allowing the sauce to thicken and the shrimp to cook through.
8. After the cooking time is complete, carefully remove the air fryer basket from Zone 1. The shrimp should be pink and opaque, and the vegetables should be crisp-tender.
9. Serve the **Shrimp and Vegetable Stir-Fry** immediately, garnished with fresh coriander.

Chapter 04: Fish & Seafood

Shrimp Fried Rice

Prep: **15** Min | Cook: **10** Min | Serves: **4**

Ingredient:

- 300g cooked rice (preferably leftover and cooled)
- 200g shrimp, peeled and deveined
- 100g frozen peas and carrots, thawed
- 1 small onion, diced
- 2 cloves garlic, minced
- 2 eggs, lightly beaten
- 2 tablespoons soy sauce
- 1 tablespoon oyster sauce
- 1 tablespoon vegetable oil
- Salt and pepper, to taste
- Spring onions, sliced, for garnish

Instruction:

1. In Zone 1 of the air fryer basket, place the shrimp, peas, carrots, diced onion, and minced garlic.
2. Drizzle the vegetable oil over the ingredients in Zone 1. Season with salt and pepper to taste. Toss to coat evenly. Select Zone 1, choose the AIR FRY program, and set the temperature to 200°C. Set the time to 5 minutes Press the START/STOP.
3. While the ingredients in Zone 1 are cooking, prepare the cooked rice separately using the stovetop or rice cooker method mentioned earlier.
4. After 5 minutes of cooking in Zone 1, carefully remove the air fryer basket. Push the ingredients in Zone 1 to one side of the basket, creating space for the eggs.
5. Pour the beaten eggs into the empty space in Zone 1. Use a spatula to scramble the eggs until cooked through.
6. Once the eggs are cooked, combine them with the ingredients in Zone 1. Add the cooked rice to Zone 1 and mix everything together. Drizzle the soy sauce and oyster sauce over the rice mixture. Toss to coat evenly.
7. Return the basket to Zone 1 and continue cooking for the remaining 5 minutes, allowing the flavors to meld and the fried rice to heat through.
8. Serve the **Shrimp Fried Rice** immediately, garnished with sliced spring onions.

Teriyaki Salmon Skewers

Prep: **20** Min | Cook: **10** Min | Serves: **4**

Ingredient:

- 500g salmon fillets, cut into 2cm cubes
- 4 tablespoons soy sauce
- 2 tablespoons honey
- 2 tablespoons rice vinegar
- 1 tablespoon sesame oil
- 2 cloves garlic, minced
- 1 teaspoon grated fresh ginger
- 1 tablespoon vegetable oil
- Spring onions, sliced, for garnish
- Sesame seeds, for garnish

Instruction:

1. In a bowl, whisk together the soy sauce, honey, rice vinegar, sesame oil, minced garlic, and grated ginger to make the teriyaki marinade.
2. Place the salmon cubes in a shallow dish or zip-top bag. Pour the teriyaki marinade over the salmon, making sure it's evenly coated. Allow the salmon to marinate for about 10 minutes.
3. Thread the marinated salmon cubes onto skewers, leaving a little space between each piece.
4. In Zone 1, place the salmon skewers. Select Zone 1, choose the AIR FRY program, and set the temperature to 200°C. Set the time to 10 minutes. Press the START/STOP button to begin cooking.
5. While the salmon skewers are cooking, in a small saucepan, heat the vegetable oil over medium heat.
6. Pour the remaining marinade into the saucepan and bring it to a simmer. Allow it to cook for about 5 minutes, or until it thickens slightly to create a glaze.
7. After 5 minutes of cooking in Zone 1, brush the salmon skewers with the teriyaki glaze, reserving some for serving and continue cooking for the remaining 5 minutes.
8. Serve the **Teriyaki Salmon Skewers** immediately, garnished with sliced spring onions and sesame seeds. Drizzle with the reserved teriyaki glaze.

Chapter 04: Fish & Seafood

Thai Red Curry Fish

Prep: **15** Min | Cook: **15** Min | Serves: **4**

Ingredient:

- 500g white fish fillets (such as cod or haddock), cut into bite-sized pieces
- 1 tablespoon vegetable oil
- 1 small onion, thinly sliced
- 2 cloves garlic, minced
- 2 tablespoons Thai red curry paste
- 400ml can of coconut milk
- 1 red bell pepper, sliced
- 1 tablespoon fish sauce
- 1 tablespoon lime juice
- 1 tablespoon brown sugar
- Fresh coriander leaves, for garnish
- Cooked rice, for serving

Instruction:

1. In Zone 1, place the fish fillet pieces. Select Zone 1, choose the AIR FRY program, and set the temperature to 200°C. Set the time to 10 minutes. Press the START/STOP button to begin cooking.
2. While the fish is cooking, in a large saucepan, heat the vegetable oil over medium heat.
3. Add the sliced onion and minced garlic to the saucepan. Sauté for 2-3 minutes until the onion becomes translucent.
4. Add the Thai red curry paste to the saucepan and cook for an additional 1-2 minutes, stirring constantly to coat the onions and garlic with the paste.
5. Pour in the coconut milk, stirring well to combine with the curry paste.
6. Add the sliced red bell pepper, fish sauce, lime juice, and brown sugar to the saucepan. Stir to incorporate the ingredients.
7. Reduce the heat to low and let the curry simmer for about 5 minutes, allowing the flavors to meld together.
8. Transfer the cooked fish from Zone 1 into the saucepan with the Thai red curry sauce. Gently stir to coat the fish with the sauce.
9. Return the saucepan to low heat and let the fish simmer in the curry sauce for an additional 2-3 minutes.
10. Serve the **Thai Red Curry Fish** over cooked rice, garnished with fresh coriander leaves.

Trout Fillets

Prep: **10** Min | Cook: **10** Min | Serves: **4**

Ingredient:

- 4 trout fillets (about 150g each)
- 2 tablespoons lemon juice
- 2 tablespoons olive oil
- 1 teaspoon dried dill
- 1 teaspoon garlic powder
- Salt and pepper, to taste
- Lemon wedges, for serving
- Fresh dill sprigs, for garnish

Instruction:

1. In a small bowl, combine the lemon juice, olive oil, dried dill, garlic powder, salt, and pepper to make a marinade.
2. Place the trout fillets in a shallow dish and pour the marinade over them, making sure they are evenly coated. Allow the fillets to marinate for about 10 minutes.
3. In Zone 1 of the air fryer basket, place the marinated trout fillets.
4. Select Zone 1, choose the AIR FRY program, and set the temperature to 200°C. Set the time to 10 minutes.
5. Press the START/STOP button to begin cooking.
6. After 10 minutes of cooking in Zone 1, carefully remove the air fryer basket. The trout fillets should be cooked through and flaky.
7. Transfer the cooked trout fillets to a serving platter.
8. Serve the **Trout Fillets** immediately, garnished with lemon wedges and fresh dill sprigs.

Chapter 04: Fish & Seafood

Tuna and Sweetcorn Quiche

Prep: **20** Min | Cook: **25** Min | Serves: **4-6**

Ingredient:

- 200g shortcrust pastry
- 1 can (160g) tuna, drained and flaked
- 150g sweetcorn kernels
- 150ml whole milk
- 150ml double cream
- 3 large eggs
- 100g grated cheddar cheese
- 1 small onion, finely chopped
- 1 tablespoon chopped fresh parsley
- Salt and pepper, to taste

Instruction:

1. Roll out the shortcrust pastry on a lightly floured surface to fit a 20cm quiche dish. Line the quiche dish with the pastry, pressing it into the edges. Trim any excess pastry.
2. In a mixing bowl, combine the drained and flaked tuna, sweetcorn kernels, chopped onion, and chopped fresh parsley. Mix well to distribute the ingredients evenly.
3. In a separate bowl, whisk together the whole milk, double cream, and eggs. Season with salt and pepper.
4. Spread the tuna and sweetcorn mixture evenly over the pastry in the quiche dish.
5. Pour the milk and egg mixture over the tuna and sweetcorn mixture, ensuring it covers the ingredients.
6. Sprinkle the grated cheddar cheese evenly over the top of the quiche.
7. Place the quiche dish in Zone 1 of the air fryer basket.
8. Select Zone 1, choose the AIR FRY program, and set the temperature to 180°C. Set the time to 25 minutes.
9. Press the START/STOP button to begin cooking.
10. After 25 minutes of cooking in Zone 1, carefully remove the air fryer basket. The quiche should be set and golden brown on top.
11. Allow the **Tuna and Sweetcorn Quiche** to cool slightly before serving. Slice into portions and serve either warm or at room temperature.

Beef Steak

Prep: **10** Min | Cook: **12** Min | Serves: **2**

Ingredient:

- 2 beef sirloin steaks (about 200g each), approximately 2cm thick
- 1 tablespoon vegetable oil
- 1 teaspoon sea salt
- 1/2 teaspoon black pepper
- 2 tablespoons unsalted butter
- 2 cloves garlic, minced
- Fresh herbs (such as thyme or rosemary), for garnish

Instruction:

1. Rub the steaks with vegetable oil, sea salt, and black pepper, ensuring they are evenly coated.
2. In Zone 1 of the air fryer basket, place the seasoned steaks in a single layer. Avoid overcrowding the basket.
3. Select Zone 1 and the AIR FRY program. Set the temperature to 200°C and the time to 6 minutes for medium-rare doneness. Adjust the cooking time based on your preference for steak doneness (e.g., 8 minutes for medium or 10 minutes for medium-well).
4. After 3 minutes, open the air fryer and flip the steaks to ensure even cooking. Close and continue cooking for the remaining time.
5. While the steaks are cooking, melt the butter in a small saucepan or microwave. Stir in the minced garlic.
6. Once the steaks are cooked to your desired level of doneness, remove them from the air fryer and let them rest for a few minutes.
7. Brush the garlic butter mixture over the steaks, allowing it to melt and coat the surface.
8. Garnish with fresh herbs, such as thyme or rosemary.
9. Serve the **Beef Steak** hot, sliced against the grain, with your favorite sides.

Chapter 05: Beef, Pork, and Lamb

Beef Stir-Fry with Vegetables

Prep: **15** Min | Cook: **15** Min | Serves: **2**

Ingredient:

- 300g beef sirloin, thinly sliced
- 2 tablespoons soy sauce
- 1 tablespoon cornstarch
- 1 tablespoon vegetable oil
- 2 cloves garlic, minced
- 1 teaspoon grated ginger
- 1 red bell pepper, sliced
- 1 green bell pepper, sliced
- 1 small onion, sliced
- 100g sugar snap peas, trimmed
- 2 tablespoons oyster sauce
- 1 tablespoon hoisin sauce
- 1/2 teaspoon sesame oil
- Fresh cilantro, for garnish
- Cooked rice or noodles, for serving

Instruction:

1. In a bowl, combine the soy sauce and cornstarch. Add the beef slices to the bowl and toss until they are evenly coated. Set aside to marinate for 10 minutes.
2. In Zone 1 of the air fryer basket, place the marinated beef slices in a single layer. Avoid overcrowding the basket.
3. Select Zone 1 and the AIR FRY program. Set the temperature to 200°C and the time to 8 minutes. Press the START/STOP button to begin cooking the beef.
4. While the beef is cooking, heat the vegetable oil in a large pan or wok over medium-high heat. Add the minced garlic and grated ginger, and stir-fry for about 1 minute until fragrant.
5. Add the sliced bell peppers, onion, and sugar snap peas to the pan. Stir-fry for 4-5 minutes until the vegetables are crisp-tender.
6. In a small bowl, whisk together the oyster sauce, hoisin sauce, and sesame oil. Pour the sauce over the stir-fried vegetables and toss to coat them evenly.
7. Once the beef slices are cooked in the air fryer, add them to the pan with the vegetables. Stir-fry for an additional 2 minutes to combine the flavors.
8. Garnish with fresh cilantro.
9. Serve the **Beef Stir-Fry with Vegetables** hot over cooked rice or noodles.

Beef and Ale Pie

Prep: **20** Min | Cook: **40** Min | Serves: **4-6**

Ingredient:

- 500g beef stewing steak, cut into bite-sized pieces
- 2 tablespoons vegetable oil
- 1 onion, chopped
- 2 carrots, peeled and diced
- 200g mushrooms, sliced
- 2 cloves of garlic, minced
- 2 tablespoons plain flour
- 300ml ale or stout
- 200ml beef stock
- 1 tablespoon Worcestershire sauce
- 1 teaspoon dried thyme
- Salt and pepper, to taste
- 500g ready-made puff pastry
- 1 egg, beaten (for egg wash)

Instruction:

1. In pan, heat the vegetable oil. Add the chopped onion, diced carrots, sliced mushrooms, and minced garlic. Cook until the vegetables have softened, about 5 minutes.
2. In Zone 1, add the beef stewing steak and cook until browned on all sides, about 5 minutes.
3. Return the cooked vegetables to Zone 1 with the beef, and sprinkle the plain flour over the mixture. Stir well to coat the meat and vegetables with the flour. Pour in the ale or stout, beef stock, Worcestershire sauce, and dried thyme. Season with salt and pepper to taste. Stir to combine all the ingredients.
4. Select Zone 1, choose the AIR FRY program, and set the temperature to 180°C. Set the time to 30 minutes. Press the START/STOP.
5. Transfer the beef and ale filling to a pie dish.
6. Roll out the puff pastry on a lightly floured surface to fit the top of the pie dish. Place the pastry over the filling, pressing the edges to seal. Brush the beaten egg over the pastry to create a golden brown crust. Place the pie dish in Zone 2. Select Zone 2, choose the AIR FRY program, and set the temperature to 180°C. Set the time to 10 minutes. Press the START/STOP.
7. Allow the **Beef and Ale Pie** to cool slightly before serving. Slice into portions and serve with your favorite side dishes.

Chapter 05: Beef, Pork, and Lamb

Beef and Guinness Pie

Prep: **20** Min | Cook: **40** Min | Serves: **4-6**

Ingredient:

- 500g beef stewing steak, cut into bite-sized pieces
- 2 tablespoons vegetable oil
- 1 onion, chopped
- 2 carrots, peeled and diced
- 200g mushrooms, sliced
- 2 cloves of garlic, minced
- 2 tablespoons plain flour
- 330ml Guinness or other stout
- 200ml beef stock
- 1 tablespoon tomato paste
- 1 tablespoon Worcestershire sauce
- 1 teaspoon dried thyme
- Salt and pepper, to taste
- 500g ready-made puff pastry
- 1 egg, beaten (for egg wash)

Instruction:

1. In pan, heat the vegetable oil. Add the chopped onion, diced carrots, sliced mushrooms, and minced garlic. Cook until the vegetables have softened, about 5 minutes.
2. Add the beef stewing steak and cook until browned on all sides, about 5 minutes.
3. Return the cooked vegetables to Zone 1 with the beef, and sprinkle the plain flour over the mixture. Stir well to coat the meat and vegetables with the flour. Pour in the Guinness or stout, beef stock, tomato paste, Worcestershire sauce, and dried thyme. Season with salt and pepper to taste. Stir to combine all the ingredients.
4. Select Zone 1, choose the AIR FRY program, and set the temperature to 180°C. Set the time to 30 minutes. Press the START/STOP button to begin cooking.
5. Transfer the beef and Guinness filling to a pie dish. Roll out the puff pastry on a lightly floured surface to fit the top of the pie dish. Place the pastry over the filling, pressing the edges to seal. Brush the beaten egg over the pastry.
6. Place the pie dish in Zone 2. Select Zone 2, choose the AIR FRY program, and set the temperature to 180°C. Set the time to 10 minutes. Press the START/STOP button to begin cooking.
7. Allow the **Beef and Guinness Pie** to cool slightly before serving. Slice into portions and serve with your favorite side dishes.

Beef Brisket

Prep: **15** Min | Cook: **60** Min | Serves: **8**

Ingredient:

- 2kg beef brisket
- 2 tablespoons vegetable oil
- 2 onions, sliced
- 4 cloves garlic, minced
- 2 carrots, sliced
- 2 celery stalks, sliced
- 500ml beef stock
- 250ml stout or dark beer
- 2 tablespoons tomato paste
- 2 tablespoons Worcestershire sauce
- 2 tablespoons brown sugar
- 2 tablespoons Dijon mustard
- 2 sprigs fresh thyme
- Salt and pepper, to taste

Instruction:

1. Season the beef brisket with salt and pepper.
2. Add the seasoned beef brisket to Zone 1. In Zone 2 of the air fryer basket, add the sliced onions, minced garlic, sliced carrots, and sliced celery.
3. Select Zone 1 and choose the ROAST program. Set the temperature to 200°C and the time to 45-60 minutes. Select MATCH. Press the START/STOP.
4. After the cooking time is complete, carefully remove the beef brisket from Zone 1 and transfer it to a cutting board. Allow it to rest for a few minutes.
5. In the meantime, remove the cooked vegetables from Zone 2 and set them aside.
6. In a saucepan, combine the beef stock, stout or dark beer, tomato paste, Worcestershire sauce, brown sugar, Dijon mustard, and fresh thyme. Simmer the sauce over medium heat for about 10 minutes to reduce and thicken.
7. Slice the rested beef brisket against the grain into thin slices.
8. Serve the sliced beef brisket with the cooked vegetables and the reduced sauce.
9. Accompany the **beef brisket** with mashed potatoes, roasted vegetables, or crusty bread.

Chapter 05: Beef, Pork, and Lamb

Beef Teriyaki Stir-Fry

Prep: **15** Min | Cook: **10** Min | Serves: **4**

Ingredient:

- 500g beef steak, thinly sliced
- 2 tablespoons vegetable oil
- 1 onion, sliced
- 2 bell peppers (any color), sliced
- 200g sugar snap peas
- 3 cloves of garlic, minced
- 2 tablespoons soy sauce
- 2 tablespoons teriyaki sauce
- 1 tablespoon honey
- 1 teaspoon cornstarch
- Salt and pepper, to taste
- Cooked rice or noodles, for serving
- Sesame seeds and chopped spring onions, for garnish

Instruction:

1. In pan, heat 1 tablespoon of vegetable oil. Add the sliced onion, bell peppers, and sugar snap peas. Stir-fry until the vegetables are crisp-tender, about 5 minutes. Set aside.
2. In another pan, heat the remaining 1 tablespoon of vegetable oil. Add the sliced beef and minced garlic. Stir-fry until the beef is browned and cooked to your desired level of doneness, about 3-4 minutes. Set aside.
3. In a small bowl, whisk together the soy sauce, teriyaki sauce, honey, cornstarch, salt, and pepper.
4. Pour the sauce mixture into Zone 1 of the air fryer basket. Add the cooked vegetables and beef to Zone 1 with the sauce. Stir well to coat the beef and vegetables with the sauce.
5. Select Zone 1, choose the AIR FRY program, and set the temperature to 180°C. Set the time to 10 minutes.
6. Press the START/STOP button to begin cooking.
7. After 10 minutes of cooking in Zone 1, carefully remove the air fryer basket. The sauce should be thickened and coating the beef and vegetables.
8. Serve the **Beef Teriyaki Stir-Fry** over cooked rice or noodles. Garnish with sesame seeds and chopped spring onions.

Roast Beef and Yorkshire Pudding

Prep: **15** Min | Cook: **60** Min | Serves: **4**

Ingredient:

For the Roast Beef:
- 1 kg beef topside joint
- 2 tablespoons olive oil
- Salt and freshly ground black pepper
- 2 garlic cloves, finely chopped
- 1 teaspoon dried thyme

For the Yorkshire Pudding:
- 140 g plain flour
- 4 large eggs
- 200 ml milk
- Pinch of salt
- Vegetable oil

Instruction:

1. Rub the beef topside joint with olive oil, garlic, thyme, salt, and pepper.
2. Place the seasoned beef in Zone 1 of the air fryer. Select Zone 1, choose the ROAST program, and set the temperature to 160°C. Set the time to 60 minutes. Press the START/STOP.
3. Use a meat thermometer to check the internal temperature - it should reach 57°C for medium-rare.
4. While the beef is cooking, whisk together the flour, eggs, milk, and a pinch of salt. Let it stand for 10 minutes.
5. Cook the Yorkshire Pudding: Add a small amount of vegetable oil into each cup of a muffin tin and place it in Zone 2 of the air fryer. Select Zone 2, AIR FRY program, set temperature to 220°C, time to 2-3 minutes.
6. After 2-3 minutes, carefully remove the hot tin, pour the batter into the cups, and place return to Zone 2 of the air fryer. Continues "AIR FRY" for 20-25 minutes until puffed and golden.
7. After cooking, remove the beef from the Zone 1 and let it rest for at least 15 minutes. Carefully remove the hot Yorkshire puddings from the Zone 2.
8. Slice the **roast beef** and serve with the hot **Yorkshire puddings**. Traditional accompaniments include gravy, roasted vegetables, and horseradish sauce.

Chapter 05: Beef, Pork, and Lamb

Beef and Broccoli

Prep: **15** Min | Cook: **12** Min | Serves: **2**

Ingredient:

- 400g beef steak, thinly sliced
- 300g broccoli florets
- 1 tablespoon vegetable oil
- 2 cloves garlic, minced
- 2 tablespoons soy sauce
- 1 tablespoon oyster sauce
- 1 tablespoon cornstarch
- 1/2 teaspoon sugar
- 1/4 teaspoon black pepper
- 1/4 teaspoon red chili flakes (optional)
- Sesame seeds, for garnish
- Spring onions, chopped, for garnish

Instruction:

1. In a small bowl, whisk together the soy sauce, oyster sauce, cornstarch, sugar, black pepper, and red chili flakes (if using). Set aside.
2. Place the sliced beef in a separate bowl and add half of the sauce mixture. Mix well to ensure the beef is coated evenly. Set aside to marinate for 10 minutes.
3. In Zone 1 of the Ninja Dual Zone Air Fryer, place the broccoli florets. Drizzle them with vegetable oil and sprinkle minced garlic over the top. Toss to coat evenly.
4. Select Zone 1, choose the AIR FRY program, and set the temperature to 200°C. Set the time to 8 minutes. Press the START/STOP button to begin cooking.
5. While cooking broccoli, in Zone 2 of the air fryer, place the marinated beef slices in a single layer. Select Zone 2, choose the AIR FRY program, and set the temperature to 200°C. Set the time to 4 minutes. Press the START/STOP button to begin cooking.
6. After 8 minutes, remove the broccoli from Zone 1 and set it aside.
7. Stir the beef slices in Zone 2, then add the remaining sauce mixture. Continue cooking for the 4 minutes or until the beef is cooked through and slightly caramelized.
8. Once cooked, transfer the beef to a serving dish and combine it with the cooked broccoli.
9. Garnish with sesame seeds and chopped spring onions.

Air-Fried Beef Schnitzel

Prep: **15** Min | Cook: **12** Min | Serves: **4**

Ingredient:

- 500g beef steak (such as rump or sirloin), thinly sliced
- 100g all-purpose flour
- 2 large eggs, beaten
- 150g breadcrumbs
- 1 teaspoon paprika
- 1 teaspoon garlic powder
- 1/2 teaspoon salt
- 1/4 teaspoon black pepper
- Vegetable oil spray

Instruction:

1. Place the all-purpose flour in a shallow dish. In a separate dish, beat the eggs. In another dish, combine the breadcrumbs, paprika, garlic powder, salt, and black pepper.
2. Dredge each beef slice in the flour, shaking off any excess. Then dip it into the beaten eggs, allowing any excess to drip off. Finally, coat it evenly with the breadcrumb mixture, pressing gently to adhere. Spray both sides of the breaded beef slices with vegetable oil spray.
3. Evenly dividing breaded beef between the two zone, ensuring they are in a single layer and not overlapping.
4. Select Zone 1, choose the AIR FRY program, and set the temperature to 200°C. Set the time to 12 minutes. Select MATCH. Press the START/STOP button to begin cooking.
5. After 6 minutes, carefully remove the air fryer basket and flip the beef schnitzels. Return the basket to the air fryer. Continue cooking for the remaining 6 minutes.
6. Carefully remove the air fryer basket and transfer the cooked beef schnitzels to a serving plate.
7. Serve the **Air-Fried Beef Schnitzel** with your choice of accompaniments, such as mashed potatoes, steamed vegetables, or a fresh salad.

Chapter 05: Beef, Pork, and Lamb

Beef Fajitas

Prep: **15** Min | Cook: **10** Min | Serves: **4**

Ingredient:

- 500g beef steak (such as sirloin or flank), thinly sliced
- 2 tablespoons vegetable oil
- 1 red bell pepper, thinly sliced
- 1 green bell pepper, thinly sliced
- 1 yellow onion, thinly sliced
- 2 cloves of garlic, minced
- 1 teaspoon ground cumin
- 1 teaspoon paprika
- 1/2 teaspoon chili powder
- 1/2 teaspoon salt
- 1/4 teaspoon black pepper
- Tortillas, for serving
- Optional toppings: sour cream, guacamole, salsa, shredded cheese, etc.

Instruction:

1. In a bowl, combine the vegetable oil, minced garlic, ground cumin, paprika, chili powder, salt, and black pepper. Mix well to make a marinade.
2. Add the thinly sliced beef steak to the marinade and toss to coat. Let it marinate for at least 10 minutes.
3. Place the sliced bell peppers and onion in Zone 1 of the air fryer basket.
4. Select Zone 1, choose the AIR FRY program, and set the temperature to 200°C. Set the time to 5 minutes.
5. Press the START/STOP button to begin cooking.
6. After 5 minutes of cooking in Zone 1, carefully remove the air fryer basket. Push the cooked peppers and onions to one side of the basket, creating space for the beef slices.
7. Place the marinated beef slices in Zone 2 of the air fryer basket.
8. Select Zone 2, choose the AIR FRY program, and set the temperature to 200°C. Set the time to 5 minutes.
9. Press the START/STOP button to begin cooking.
10. After the remaining 5 minutes of cooking, carefully remove the air fryer basket. The beef should be cooked to your desired doneness, and the peppers and onions should be tender and slightly charred.
11. Serve the **Beef Fajitas** in warm tortillas, along with the cooked peppers and onions. Add your favorite toppings, such as sour cream, guacamole, salsa, or shredded cheese.

Beef Satay Skewers

Prep: **20** Min | Cook: **8** Min | Serves: **4**

Ingredient:

For the Marinade:
- 500g beef sirloin, thinly sliced
- 2 cloves of garlic, minced
- 1 teaspoon ground cumin
- 1 teaspoon ground coriander
- 1/2 teaspoon turmeric powder
- Skewers, soaked in water for 30 minutes
- 3 tsp soy sauce
- 2 tsp vegetable oil
- 2 tsp honey
- 1 tsp lime juice

For the Peanut Sauce:
- 100g peanut butter
- 2 tablespoons soy sauce
- 1 tablespoon honey
- 1 tablespoon lime juice
- 1 clove of garlic, minced
- 1/2 teaspoon chili flakes (optional)
- Water, as needed to adjust consistency

Instruction:

1. In a bowl, combine the soy sauce, vegetable oil, honey, lime juice, minced garlic, ground cumin, ground coriander, and turmeric powder. Mix well to make the marinade.
2. Add the thinly sliced beef sirloin to the marinade and toss to coat. Let it marinate for at least 15 minutes, or refrigerate for up to 1 hour for more flavor.
3. Thread the marinated beef slices onto the soaked skewers.
4. Place the beef skewers in Zone 1 of the air fryer basket.
5. Select Zone 1, choose the AIR FRY program, and set the temperature to 200°C. Set the time to 8 minutes.
6. Press the START/STOP button to begin cooking.
7. While the beef skewers are cooking, prepare the peanut sauce. In a small bowl, whisk together the peanut butter, soy sauce, honey, lime juice, minced garlic, and chili flakes (if using). Add water gradually to adjust the consistency of the sauce to your liking.
8. After 8 minutes of cooking in Zone 1, carefully remove the air fryer basket. The beef skewers should be cooked through and nicely charred.
9. Serve the **Beef Satay skewers** with the peanut sauce on the side. You can also serve it with steamed rice and a side of cucumber and onion salad.

Chapter 05: Beef, Pork, and Lamb

Beef Kebabs

Prep: **20** Min | Cook: **12** Min | Serves: **4**

Ingredient:

- 500g beef steak (such as sirloin or rump), cut into 2.5cm cubes
- 1 red bell pepper, cut into 2.5cm pieces
- 1 green bell pepper, cut into 2.5cm pieces
- 1 yellow onion, cut into 2.5cm pieces
- 2 tablespoons olive oil
- 2 tablespoons Worcestershire sauce
- 2 cloves of garlic, minced
- 1 teaspoon dried oregano
- 1 teaspoon paprika
- 1/2 teaspoon salt
- 1/4 teaspoon black pepper
- Skewers, soaked in water for 30 minutes

Instruction:

1. In a bowl, combine the olive oil, Worcestershire sauce, minced garlic, dried oregano, paprika, salt, and black pepper. Mix well to make a marinade.
2. Add the beef cubes to the marinade and toss to coat. Let it marinate for at least 15 minutes, or refrigerate for up to 1 hour for more flavor.
3. Thread the marinated beef cubes, bell pepper pieces, and onion pieces onto the soaked skewers, alternating between the ingredients.
4. Place the beef kebabs in Zone 1 of the air fryer basket.
5. Select Zone 1, choose the AIR FRY program, and set the temperature to 200°C. Set the time to 12 minutes.
6. Press the START/STOP button to begin cooking.
7. After 6 minutes of cooking in Zone 1, carefully remove the air fryer basket and flip the kebabs. Return the basket to the air fryer.
8. Continue cooking for the remaining 6 minutes or until the beef is cooked to your desired level of doneness, and the vegetables are tender and slightly charred.
9. Carefully remove the air fryer basket and transfer the cooked beef kebabs to a serving plate.
10. Serve the **Beef Kebabs** with your choice of accompaniments, such as pita bread, tzatziki sauce, and a side salad.

Pork and Apple Burgers

Prep: 15 Min | Cook: 10 Min | Serves: 4

Ingredient:

- 500g ground pork
- 1 small apple, grated
- 1 small onion, finely chopped
- 2 cloves of garlic, minced
- 1 teaspoon dried sage
- 1/2 teaspoon dried thyme
- 1/2 teaspoon salt
- 1/4 teaspoon black pepper
- Burger buns, for serving
- Optional toppings: lettuce, tomato, cheese, mayonnaise, etc.

...▶ *Instruction:*

1. In a large bowl, combine the ground pork, grated apple, finely chopped onion, minced garlic, dried sage, dried thyme, salt, and black pepper. Mix well until all the ingredients are evenly incorporated.
2. Divide the mixture into four equal portions and shape each portion into a patty.
3. Place the pork patties in Zone 1 of the air fryer basket.
4. Select Zone 1, choose the AIR FRY program, and set the temperature to 200°C. Set the time to 10 minutes.
5. Press the START/STOP button to begin cooking.
6. After 5 minutes of cooking in Zone 1, carefully remove the air fryer basket and flip the burgers. Return the basket to the air fryer.
7. Continue cooking for the remaining 5 minutes or until the burgers are cooked through and nicely browned.
8. Carefully remove the air fryer basket and transfer the cooked pork and apple burgers to burger buns.
9. Add your desired toppings, such as lettuce, tomato, cheese, and mayonnaise.
10. Enjoy your delicious **Pork and Apple Burgers**!

Chapter 05: Beef, Pork, and Lamb

Pulled Pork Sliders

Prep: 30 Min | Cook: 20 Min | Serves: 4

Ingredient:

For the Pulled Pork:
- 800g pork shoulder, boneless
- 3 cloves of garlic, minced
- 2 tablespoons brown sugar
- 2 tablespoons tomato paste
- 2 tablespoons Worcestershire sauce
- 1 tablespoon apple cider vinegar
- 1 teaspoon smoked paprika
- 1 teaspoon mustard powder
- 1/2 teaspoon salt
- 1/4 teaspoon black pepper
- 240ml chicken or vegetable broth
- 1 tsp olive oil
- 1 onion, chopped

For the Sliders:
- Mini slider buns
- Coleslaw, for topping (optional)
- Pickles, for topping (optional)

...▶ *Instruction:*

1. In a large skillet, heat the olive oil over medium heat. Add the chopped onion and minced garlic, and sauté until translucent and fragrant.
2. Add the brown sugar, tomato paste, Worcestershire sauce, apple cider vinegar, smoked paprika, mustard powder, salt, and black pepper to the skillet. Stir well to combine.
3. Place the pork shoulder in the skillet and coat it with the sauce mixture. Pour in the chicken or vegetable broth.
4. Cover the skillet and let the pork simmer over low heat for 1 hour or until the meat is tender and easily pulls apart.
5. Once the pork is cooked, remove it from the skillet and transfer it to a cutting board. Use two forks to shred the meat.
6. Place the shredded pork in Zone 1 of the air fryer basket.
7. Select Zone 1, choose the AIR FRY program, and set the temperature to 160°C. Set the time to 20 minutes.
8. Press the START/STOP button to begin cooking.
9. After 10 minutes of cooking in Zone 1, carefully remove the air fryer basket and stir the shredded pork to ensure even browning. Return the basket to the air fryer.
10. Continue cooking for the remaining 10 minutes or until the pulled pork is crispy on the edges.
11. Carefully remove the air fryer basket and assemble the pulled pork sliders. Place a spoonful of the crispy **pulled pork** on each slider bun. Top with coleslaw and pickles, if desired.

Pork and Mushroom Pie

Prep: 20 Min | Cook: 25 Min | Serves: 4

Ingredient:

- 500g pork shoulder, diced
- 200g mushrooms, sliced
- 1 onion, chopped
- 2 cloves of garlic, minced
- 2 tablespoons olive oil
- 2 tablespoons plain flour
- 300ml chicken or vegetable stock
- 150ml double cream
- 1 teaspoon dried thyme
- Salt and pepper to taste
- 1 sheet of ready-rolled puff pastry
- 1 egg, beaten (for egg wash)

Instruction:

1. In a large skillet, heat the olive oil over medium heat. Add the chopped onion and minced garlic, and sauté until the onion is soft and translucent. Add the diced pork and cook until browned on all sides. Add the sliced mushrooms and cook for an additional 3-4 minutes until softened.
2. Sprinkle the flour over the pork and mushrooms, stirring to coat everything evenly. Gradually pour in the chicken or vegetable stock while stirring constantly. Pour in the double cream and add the dried thyme. Stir well to combine. Season with salt and pepper to taste.
3. Roll out the puff pastry sheet on a lightly floured surface to fit the size of your pie dish.
4. Transfer the pork and mushroom mixture to a pie dish. Place the puff pastry sheet on top, pressing the edges to seal. Brush the top of the pastry with beaten egg.
5. Place the pie dish in Zone 1. Select Zone 1, choose the AIR FRY program, and set the temperature to 180°C for 25 minutes. Press the START/STOP.
6. After 15 minutes, carefully remove the air fryer basket and cover the pie with aluminum foil to prevent over-browning.
7. Enjoy your delicious **Pork and Mushroom Pie**!

Chapter 05: Beef, Pork, and Lamb

Pork Satay Skewers

Prep: 25 Min | Cook: 15 Min | Serves: 4

Ingredient:

- 500g pork tenderloin, cut into thin strips
- 3 tablespoons soy sauce
- 2 tablespoons peanut butter
- 2 tablespoons honey
- 1 tablespoon lime juice
- 2 cloves garlic, minced
- 1 teaspoon curry powder
- 1/2 teaspoon ground cumin
- 1/4 teaspoon turmeric
- Salt and pepper to taste
- Wooden skewers, soaked in water

Instruction:

1. In a mixing bowl, combine the soy sauce, peanut butter, honey, lime juice, minced garlic, curry powder, ground cumin, turmeric, salt, and pepper. Mix well to make the marinade.
2. Add the pork strips to the marinade, tossing to coat them evenly. Let the pork marinate for at least 15 minutes.
3. Thread the marinated pork strips onto the soaked wooden skewers.
4. Place the skewers in Zone 1 of the Ninja Dual Zone Air Fryer.
5. Select Zone 1, choose the AIR FRY program, and set the temperature to 200°C. Set the time to 15 minutes.
6. Press the START/STOP button to begin cooking.
7. After 7 minutes, flipt to ensure even cooking. Continue cooking until the pork is cooked through and slightly charred.
8. Once cooked, remove the **Pork Satay Skewers** from the air fryer and let them cool slightly before serving.

Pork Belly Bites

Prep: **15** Min | Cook: **30** Min | Serves: **4**

Ingredient:

- 500g pork belly, skin-on, cut into bite-sized pieces
- 2 tablespoons vegetable oil
- 2 tablespoons soy sauce
- 2 tablespoons honey
- 1 tablespoon apple cider vinegar
- 1 tablespoon tomato ketchup
- 1 tablespoon Worcestershire sauce
- 1 teaspoon smoked paprika
- 1/2 teaspoon garlic powder
- 1/2 teaspoon onion powder
- Salt and pepper to taste
- Chopped spring onions, for garnish (optional)

Instruction:

1. In a bowl, combine the vegetable oil, soy sauce, honey, apple cider vinegar, tomato ketchup, Worcestershire sauce, smoked paprika, garlic powder, onion powder, salt, and pepper. Mix well to make a marinade.
2. Place the pork belly bites in the marinade, ensuring that each piece is coated evenly. Let the pork marinate for at least 10 minutes, or refrigerate for up to 4 hours for enhanced flavor.
3. Place the marinated pork belly bites in Zone 1 of the air fryer basket.
4. Select Zone 1, choose the AIR FRY program, and set the temperature to 200°C. Set the time to 30 minutes.
5. Press the START/STOP button to begin cooking.
6. After 15 minutes of cooking in Zone 1, carefully remove the air fryer basket and flip the pork belly bites for even browning. Return the basket to the air fryer.
7. Continue cooking for the remaining 15 minutes or until the pork belly bites are crispy and golden.
8. Garnish with chopped spring onions, if desired, and serve hot as a delicious appetizer or snack. Enjoy your delicious **Pork Belly Bites**!

Chapter 05: Beef, Pork, and Lamb

Pork and Cabbage Dumplings

Prep: **30** Min | Cook: **15** Min

Serves: **30 Dumplings**

Ingredient:

- 150g cabbage, finely chopped
- 2 spring onions, finely chopped
- 2 cloves of garlic, minced
- 1 teaspoon grated ginger
- 1 tablespoon soy sauce
- 1 tablespoon oyster sauce
- 1/4 teaspoon white pepper
- 30 round dumpling wrappers
- Water (for sealing the dumplings)
- Vegetable oil (for brushing)
- 1/2 teaspoon sugar
- 250g minced pork
- 1 tsp sesame oil

For the Dipping Sauce:

- 2 tablespoons soy sauce
- 1 tablespoon rice vinegar
- 1 teaspoon sesame oil
- Chopped spring onions (for garnish, optional)

Instruction:

1. In a large bowl, combine the minced pork, chopped cabbage, spring onions, minced garlic, grated ginger, soy sauce, oyster sauce, sesame oil, sugar, and white pepper. Mix well until all the ingredients are evenly incorporated.
2. Place a small amount of the filling (about 1 teaspoon) in the center of a dumpling wrapper. Dip your finger in water and moisten the edges of the wrapper.
3. Fold the dumpling wrapper in half, forming a semicircle shape, and press the edges together to seal. Pleat the edges if desired for a decorative look. Repeat this process until all the filling is used.
4. Evenly dividing dumplings between the two zone, making sure they are not touching each other.
5. Select Zone 1, choose the AIR FRY program, and set the temperature to 180°C. Set the time to 15 minutes. Select MATCH. Press the START/STOP button to begin cooking.
6. After 8 minutes, carefully remove the air fryer basket and brush the dumplings with vegetable oil to promote browning. Return the basket to the air fryer.
7. While the dumplings are cooking, prepare the dipping sauce. In a small bowl, mix together the soy sauce, rice vinegar, and sesame oil. Carefully remove the air fryer basket and transfer the cooked dumplings to a serving plate. Garnish with chopped spring onions, if desired. Serve the **pork and cabbage dumplings** hot with the dipping sauce on the side.

Pork and Black Pudding Scotch Eggs

Prep: 20 Min | Cook: 20 Min

Serves: **4 Scotch eggs**

Ingredient:

- 4 large eggs
- 250g pork sausage meat
- 100g black pudding, crumbled
- 50g breadcrumbs
- 1 tablespoon chopped fresh parsley
- 1/2 teaspoon dried thyme
- Salt and pepper to taste
- Flour, for dusting
- Vegetable oil, for brushing

Instruction:

1. Place the eggs in a saucepan and cover them with cold water. Bring the water to a boil, then reduce the heat and simmer the eggs for 6 minutes. Remove the eggs from the saucepan and place them in a bowl of ice water to cool completely. Once cooled, carefully peel the eggs.
2. In a bowl, combine the pork sausage meat, crumbled black pudding, breadcrumbs, chopped fresh parsley, dried thyme, salt, and pepper. Mix well.
3. Divide the sausage and black pudding mixture into 4 equal portions. Flatten each portion into a thin patty.
4. Place a peeled egg in the center of each patty and gently wrap the meat mixture around the egg, ensuring it is completely covered.
5. Dust each Scotch egg with flour, shaking off any excess.
6. Place the Scotch eggs in Zone 1 of the Ninja Dual Zone Air Fryer, making sure they are not touching each other.
7. Select Zone 1, choose the AIR FRY program, and set the temperature to 180°C. Set the time to 20 minutes. Press the START/STOP button to begin cooking.
8. Transfer the cooked **Pork and Black Pudding Scotch Eggs** to a serving plate. Let them cool slightly before serving.

Chapter 05: Beef, Pork, and Lamb

Pork Stuffed Bell Peppers

Prep: 20 Min | Cook: 25 Min

Serves: **4 stuffed bell peppers**

Ingredient:

- 4 large bell peppers (assorted colors)
- 500g ground pork
- 1 small onion, finely chopped
- 2 cloves of garlic, minced
- 1 medium carrot, finely grated
- 100g mushrooms, finely chopped
- 100g cooked rice
- 2 tablespoons tomato paste
- 1 teaspoon Worcestershire sauce
- 1 teaspoon dried oregano
- 1/2 teaspoon dried thyme
- Salt and pepper to taste
- Grated cheese, for topping (optional)

Instruction:

1. Cut off the tops of the bell peppers and remove the seeds and membranes. Rinse the peppers under cold water and set them aside.
2. In a large skillet, heat a little oil over medium heat. Add the ground pork, chopped onion, and minced garlic. Cook until the pork is browned and the onion is softened.
3. Add the grated carrot and chopped mushrooms to the skillet. Cook for an additional 3-4 minutes or until the vegetables are tender.
4. Stir in the cooked rice, tomato paste, Worcestershire sauce, dried oregano, dried thyme, salt, and pepper. Mix well until all the ingredients are combined. Remove the skillet from the heat.
5. Stuff each bell pepper with the pork and rice mixture, pressing it in firmly. Place the stuffed bell peppers in Zone 1. Select Zone 1, choose the AIR FRY program, and set the temperature to 180°C. Set the time to 25 minutes. Press the START/STOP.
6. After 15 minutes, carefully remove the air fryer basket and, if desired, sprinkle grated cheese on top of each stuffed bell pepper. Return the basket to the air fryer.
7. Continue cooking for the remaining 10 minutes or until the bell peppers are tender and the cheese is melted and slightly golden.
8. Carefully remove the air fryer basket and transfer the cooked **stuffed bell peppers** to a serving plate.

Pork and Vegetable Spring Rolls

Prep: **30** Min | Cook: **15** Min

Serves: **12 spring rolls**

Ingredient:

- 100g shredded cabbage
- 1 carrot, julienned
- 2 spring onions, thinly sliced
- 2 cloves of garlic, minced
- 1 teaspoon grated ginger
- 1 tablespoon soy sauce
- 1 tablespoon cornstarch
- 1/2 teaspoon sugar
- 1/4 teaspoon white pepper
- 12 spring roll wrappers
- Water (for sealing the spring rolls)
- Vegetable oil (for brushing)
- 200g minced pork
- 100g bean sprouts

Dipping Sauce:
- 3 tsp soy sauce
- 1 tsp rice vinegar
- 1 tsp sesame oil

Instruction:

1. In a large bowl, combine the minced pork, bean sprouts, shredded cabbage, carrot, spring onions, minced garlic, grated ginger, soy sauce, cornstarch, sugar, and white pepper. Mix well until all the ingredients are evenly incorporated.
2. Place a spring roll wrapper on a clean surface. Spoon about 2 tablespoons of the pork and vegetable mixture onto the lower half of the wrapper.
3. Fold the bottom edge of the wrapper over the filling, then fold in the sides. Roll up tightly, using a bit of water to seal the edges. Repeat this process until all the filling is used.
4. Evenly dividing spring rolls between the two zone, making sure they are not touching each other Select Zone 1, choose the AIR FRY program, and set the temperature to 180°C. Set the time to 15 minutes. Select MATCH. Press the START/STOP button to begin cooking.
5. After 8 minutes, carefully remove the air fryer basket and brush the spring rolls with vegetable oil to promote browning. Until the spring rolls are golden and crispy.
6. While the spring rolls are cooking, prepare the dipping sauce. In a small bowl, mix together the soy sauce, rice vinegar, and sesame oil.
7. Garnish with chopped spring onions. Serve the **pork and vegetable spring rolls** hot with the dipping sauce on the side.

Chapter 05: Beef, Pork, and Lamb

Lamb Souvlaki Skewers

Prep: **20** Min | Cook: **12** Min | Serves: **4 skewers**

Ingredient:

- 500g lamb leg meat, cut into cubes
- 2 tablespoons olive oil
- 2 tablespoons lemon juice
- 2 cloves of garlic, minced
- 1 teaspoon dried oregano
- 1/2 teaspoon salt
- 1/4 teaspoon black pepper
- 1 red onion, cut into chunks
- 1 red bell pepper, cut into chunks
- 1 green bell pepper, cut into chunks
- Wooden skewers, soaked in water

Instruction:

1. In a bowl, combine the olive oil, lemon juice, minced garlic, dried oregano, salt, and black pepper. Mix well to create the marinade.
2. Add the lamb cubes to the marinade and toss until they are well coated. Cover the bowl and let the lamb marinate in the refrigerator for at least 1 hour, or overnight for best results.
3. Thread the marinated lamb cubes onto the soaked wooden skewers, alternating with chunks of red onion and bell peppers.
4. Evenly dividing skewers between the two zone, making sure they are not touching each other.
5. Select Zone 1, choose the AIR FRY program, and set the temperature to 200°C. Set the time to 12 minutes. Select MATCH. Press the START/STOP button to begin cooking.
6. After 6 minutes, carefully remove the air fryer basket and flip the skewers to ensure even cooking. Return the basket to the air fryer.
7. Continue cooking for the remaining 6 minutes or until the lamb is cooked to your desired level of doneness and the vegetables are slightly charred.
8. Carefully remove the air fryer basket and transfer the cooked lamb souvlaki skewers to a serving plate.
9. Serve the **lamb souvlaki skewers** hot with some tzatziki sauce and a side of Greek salad or pita bread.

Lamb Curry

Prep: 20 Min | Cook: 45 Min | Serves: 4

Ingredient:

- 500g lamb shoulder, cut into bite-sized pieces
- 2 tablespoons vegetable oil
- 1 onion, finely chopped
- 3 cloves of garlic, minced
- 1 tablespoon grated ginger
- 2 tablespoons curry powder
- 1 teaspoon ground cumin
- 1 teaspoon ground coriander
- 1/2 teaspoon turmeric
- 1/4 teaspoon cayenne pepper
- 400ml canned chopped tomatoes
- 200ml coconut milk
- 1 tablespoon tomato paste
- 1 tablespoon sugar
- Salt, to taste
- Fresh coriander leaves, for garnish (optional)

Instruction:

1. In a frying pan, heat the vegetable oil and add the chopped onions. Cook for 3-4 minutes until the onions are soft and lightly golden. Add the minced garlic and grated ginger and cook for another 1-2 minutes until fragrant.
2. In a bowl, combine the curry powder, ground cumin, ground coriander, turmeric, and cayenne pepper (if using) to make a spice mixture.
3. Add the spice mixture to the pan, stirring well to coat the onions, garlic, and ginger.
4. Add the lamb pieces and cook for 5-6 minutes, stirring occasionally, until the lamb is browned on all sides.
5. In Zone 1, place the lamb and add the canned chopped tomatoes, coconut milk, tomato paste, sugar, and salt. Stir well to combine all the ingredients.
6. Select Zone 1, choose the AIR FRY program, and set the temperature to 150°C. Set the time to 45 minutes.
7. Press the START/STOP button to begin cooking.
8. After 45 minutes of slow cooking in Zone 1, carefully remove the air fryer basket and transfer the lamb curry to a serving dish.
9. Garnish with fresh coriander leaves, if desired.
10. Serve the **lamb curry** hot with steamed rice or naan bread.

Chapter 05: Beef, Pork, and Lamb

Lamb and Mint Meatloaf

Prep: 15 Min | Cook: 30 Min | Serves: 4 wraps

Ingredient:

- 500g lamb mince
- 1 onion, finely chopped
- 2 cloves of garlic, minced
- 2 tablespoons fresh mint leaves, finely chopped
- 1 tablespoon Worcestershire sauce
- 1 teaspoon dried oregano
- 1/2 teaspoon salt
- 1/4 teaspoon black pepper
- 1 egg, beaten
- 60g breadcrumbs
- 2 tablespoons tomato ketchup

Instruction:

1. In a large bowl, combine the lamb mince, chopped onion, minced garlic, fresh mint leaves, Worcestershire sauce, dried oregano, salt, black pepper, beaten egg, and breadcrumbs. Mix well until all the ingredients are evenly incorporated.
2. Shape the lamb mixture into a loaf shape and place it in Zone 1 of the air fryer basket.
3. Select Zone 1, choose the ROAST program, and set the temperature to 180°C. Set the time to 30 minutes.
4. Press the START/STOP button to begin cooking.
5. After 15 minutes of cooking in Zone 1, carefully remove the air fryer basket and brush the top of the meatloaf with tomato ketchup for added flavor and a glaze. Return the basket to the air fryer.
6. Continue cooking for the remaining 15 minutes or until the lamb meatloaf is cooked through and nicely browned on the outside.
7. Carefully remove the air fryer basket and transfer the cooked lamb and mint meatloaf to a serving plate.
8. Let the meatloaf rest for a few minutes before slicing.
9. Serve the **lamb and mint meatloaf** hot with your favorite sides, such as mashed potatoes and steamed vegetables.

Lamb Kofta Kebabs

Prep: **20** Min | Cook: **12** Min | Serves: **4**

Ingredient:

- 500g lamb mince
- 1 onion, finely chopped
- 2 cloves of garlic, minced
- 2 tablespoons fresh parsley, finely chopped
- 1 teaspoon ground cumin
- 1 teaspoon ground coriander
- 1/2 teaspoon ground paprika
- 1/2 teaspoon salt
- 1/4 teaspoon black pepper
- 1 tablespoon vegetable oil

Instruction:

1. In a large bowl, combine the lamb mince, chopped onion, minced garlic, fresh parsley, ground cumin, ground coriander, ground paprika, salt, and black pepper. Mix well until all the ingredients are evenly incorporated.
2. Divide the lamb mixture into 8 portions and shape each portion into a cylindrical kebab shape.
3. Evenly dividing lamb kofta kebabs between the two zone.
4. Select Zone 1, choose the ROAST program, and set the temperature to 200°C. Set the time to 12 minutes. Select MATCH. Press the START/STOP button to begin cooking.
5. After 6 minutes, carefully remove the air fryer basket and brush the kebabs with vegetable oil to add a golden crust. Return the basket to the air fryer.
6. Continue cooking for the remaining 6 minutes or until the lamb kofta kebabs are cooked through and nicely browned on the outside.
7. Carefully remove the air fryer basket and transfer the cooked lamb kofta kebabs to a serving plate.
8. Serve the **lamb kofta kebabs** hot with pita bread, tzatziki sauce, and a side salad.

Chapter 05: Beef, Pork, and Lamb

Lamb and Potato Hash

Prep: **15** Min | Cook: **25** Min | Serves: **4**

Ingredient:

- 500g lamb leg steaks, diced
- 500g potatoes, peeled and cubed
- 1 onion, diced
- 2 cloves garlic, minced
- 2 tablespoons vegetable oil
- 1 teaspoon dried rosemary
- 1 teaspoon dried thyme
- Salt and pepper, to taste
- Fresh parsley, chopped (for garnish)

Instruction:

1. In a large bowl, combine the diced lamb, cubed potatoes, diced onion, minced garlic, vegetable oil, dried rosemary, dried thyme, salt, and pepper. Toss until everything is well coated.
2. Divide the mixture evenly between Zone 1 and Zone 2. Spread it out in a single layer for even cooking.
3. Select Zone 1, choose the Air Fry program, and set the temperature to 180°C. Set the time to 20-25 minutes to cook the lamb and potato hash. Select MATCH. Press the START/STOP button to begin cooking.
4. Halfway through the cooking time, pause the air fryer and carefully shake or toss the contents in both zones to ensure even browning.
5. Resume cooking until the lamb is cooked through, the potatoes are golden and crispy, and the onions are tender.
6. Once cooked, carefully remove the lamb and potato hash from the air fryer.
7. Garnish with freshly chopped parsley.
8. Serve the **lamb and potato hash** hot as a delicious and satisfying meal.

Lamb Chilli Con Carne

Prep: **15** Min | Cook: **40** Min | Serves: **4**

Ingredient:

- 500g minced lamb
- 1 onion, finely chopped
- 2 cloves of garlic, minced
- 1 red bell pepper, diced
- 1 green bell pepper, diced
- 1 can (400g) kidney beans, drained and rinsed
- 1 can (400g) chopped tomatoes
- 2 tablespoons tomato paste
- 1 teaspoon ground cumin
- 1 teaspoon ground paprika
- 1/2 teaspoon ground cinnamon
- 1/2 teaspoon dried oregano
- 1/4 teaspoon black pepper
- 2 tablespoons vegetable oil
- 1/2 teaspoon sugar
- 1/2 teaspoon salt

Instruction:

1. In a frying pan, heat the vegetable oil and add the chopped onions. Cook for 3-4 minutes until the onions are soft and lightly golden. Add the minced garlic and cook for another 1-2 minutes until fragrant. Add the minced lamb and cook for 5-6 minutes, stirring occasionally, until the lamb is browned.
2. In Zone 1, place the lamb and add the diced red and green bell peppers, kidney beans, chopped tomatoes, tomato paste, ground cumin, ground paprika, ground cinnamon, dried oregano, sugar, salt, and black pepper. Stir well to combine all the ingredients.
3. Select Zone 1, choose the ROAST program, and set the temperature to 180°C. Set the time to 30 minutes.
4. Press the START/STOP button to begin cooking.
5. After 15 minutes of air roasting in Zone 1, carefully remove the air fryer basket and give the lamb chilli con carne a good stir. Return the basket to the air fryer.
6. Continue cooking for the remaining 15 minutes or until the lamb is cooked through and the flavors are well combined.
7. Carefully remove the air fryer basket and transfer the cooked lamb chilli con carne to a serving dish.
8. Serve the **lamb chilli con carne** hot with rice or tortilla chips.

Chapter 05: Beef, Pork, and Lamb

Lamb Shawarma

Prep: **15** Min | Cook: **30** Min | Serves: **4**

Ingredient:

- 500g boneless lamb leg or shoulder, thinly sliced
- 2 tablespoons olive oil
- 2 tablespoons lemon juice
- 2 cloves of garlic, minced
- 1 teaspoon ground cumin
- 1 teaspoon ground paprika
- 1/2 teaspoon ground coriander
- 1/2 teaspoon ground cinnamon
- 1/2 teaspoon ground turmeric
- 1/2 teaspoon salt
- 1/4 teaspoon black pepper
- 4 pita breads
- Toppings: sliced tomatoes, sliced cucumbers, sliced red onions, shredded lettuce, tahini sauce, yogurt sauce

Instruction:

1. In a bowl, combine the olive oil, lemon juice, minced garlic, ground cumin, ground paprika, ground coriander, ground cinnamon, ground turmeric, salt, and black pepper. Mix well to make a marinade.
2. Place the thinly sliced lamb in a resealable bag or a bowl. Pour the marinade over the lamb slices, ensuring they are well coated. If time permits, marinate the lamb in the refrigerator for 1 hour to enhance the flavors. If not, proceed to the next step.
3. In Zone 1, place the marinated lamb slices in a single layer. Reserve any remaining marinade. Select Zone 1, choose the ROAST program, and set the temperature to 200°C. Set the time to 30 minutes. Press the START/STOP button to begin cooking.
4. After 15 minutes of air roasting in Zone 1, carefully remove the air fryer basket and brush the lamb slices with the reserved marinade for added flavor. Return the basket to the air fryer.
5. Carefully remove the air fryer basket and transfer the cooked lamb shawarma slices to a serving plate.
6. Warm the pita breads in the air fryer for about 1 minute, until slightly toasted.
7. Fill each warmed pita bread with the cooked lamb slices and desired toppings such as sliced tomatoes, sliced cucumbers, sliced red onions, shredded lettuce, tahini sauce, and yogurt sauce.
8. Serve the **Lamb Shawarma** immediately and enjoy!

Arancini Balls

Prep: **30** Min | Cook: **12** Min | Serves: **4**

Ingredient:

- 200g risotto rice
- 500ml vegetable stock
- 1 small onion, finely chopped
- 1 garlic clove, minced
- 50g grated Parmesan cheese
- 50g mozzarella cheese, diced
- 2 eggs, beaten
- 80g breadcrumbs
- Olive oil spray

Instruction:

1. In a saucepan, bring the vegetable stock to a boil. Add the risotto rice and cook according to the package instructions until al dente.
2. In a frying pan, heat a little oil over medium heat. Add the finely chopped onion and minced garlic. Sauté until the onion is soft and translucent. Remove from heat and allow it to cool.
3. In a large mixing bowl, combine the cooked risotto rice, sautéed onion and garlic, grated Parmesan cheese, and diced mozzarella cheese. Mix well. Take a small handful of the rice mixture and shape it into a ball, approximately 5cm in diameter.
4. Place the beaten eggs in one bowl and the breadcrumbs in another bowl. Dip each rice ball into the beaten eggs, ensuring it is coated evenly. Then, roll it in the breadcrumbs, pressing gently to adhere the breadcrumbs to the surface.
5. Place the coated arancini balls in Zone 1 of the Ninja Dual Zone Air Fryer, ensuring they are arranged in a single layer.
6. Select Zone 1, choose the AIR FRY program, and set the temperature to 200°C for 12 minutes. Press the START/STOP.
7. After 6 minutes of cooking, carefully open the air fryer and shake the basket to turn the arancini balls. Continue cooking for the remaining 6 minutes.
8. Serve the **Arancini Balls** as a delicious appetizer or as part of a main course.

Chapter 06: Appetizers & Snacks

Avocado Fries

Prep: **15** Min | Cook: **10** Min | Serves: **4**

Ingredient:

- 2 ripe avocados
- 100g plain flour
- 2 eggs, beaten
- 100g breadcrumbs
- 1/2 tsp paprika
- 1/2 tsp garlic powder
- Salt and pepper to taste
- Olive oil spray

Instruction:

1. Cut the avocados in half lengthwise, remove the pit, and peel off the skin. Slice each avocado half into thick fries, about 1cm wide.
2. In a shallow bowl, combine the plain flour with a pinch of salt and pepper. In another shallow bowl, whisk together the beaten eggs. In a third shallow bowl, mix the breadcrumbs with paprika, garlic powder, salt, and pepper.
3. Dip each avocado fry into the flour mixture, shaking off any excess. Then, dip it into the beaten eggs, allowing any excess to drip off. Finally, coat it in the breadcrumb mixture, pressing gently to adhere the breadcrumbs to the surface. Repeat with the remaining avocado fries.
4. Place the coated avocado fries in Zone 1 of the Ninja Dual Zone Air Fryer, ensuring they are arranged in a single layer.
5. Select Zone 1, choose the AIR FRY program, and set the temperature to 200°C. Set the time to 10 minutes.
6. Press the START/STOP button to begin cooking.
7. After 5 minutes of cooking, carefully open the air fryer and shake the basket or use tongs to turn the avocado fries for even cooking.
8. Continue cooking for the remaining 5 minutes or until the avocado fries are golden brown and crispy.
9. Once cooked, remove the Avocado Fries from the air fryer and let them cool slightly. Serve the **Avocado Fries** as a delicious and healthy appetizer or snack.

Bruschetta

Prep: **10** Min | Cook: **5** Min | Serves: **4**

Ingredient:

- 4 slices of baguette, about 1 cm thick
- 200g ripe tomatoes, diced
- 1 garlic clove, minced
- 10g fresh basil leaves, chopped
- 15g red onion, finely chopped
- 15ml extra virgin olive oil
- Salt and pepper to taste

Instruction:

1. In a bowl, combine the diced tomatoes, minced garlic, chopped basil leaves, finely chopped red onion, extra virgin olive oil, salt, and pepper. Mix well to combine.
2. Place the baguette slices in Zone 1 and Zone 2 of the Ninja Dual Zone Air Fryer, ensuring they are arranged in a single layer.
3. Select Zone 1, choose the AIR FRY program, and set the temperature to 180°C. Set the time to 5 minutes. Select MATCH.
4. Press the START/STOP button to begin cooking.
5. After 2 minutes of cooking, carefully open the air fryer and flip the baguette slices for even browning.
6. Continue cooking for the remaining 3 minutes or until the baguette slices turn golden and crispy.
7. Once cooked, remove the baguette slices from the air fryer and let them cool slightly.
8. Spoon the tomato mixture onto the toasted side of each baguette slice, allowing the flavors to meld together.
9. Serve the **Bruschetta** warm as an appetizer or snack.

Chapter 06: Appetizers & Snacks

Caprese Skewers

Prep: **15** Min | Cook: **5** Min | Serves: **4**

Ingredient:

- 200g cherry tomatoes
- 200g fresh mozzarella cheese, cut into bite-sized pieces
- 15g fresh basil leaves
- 15ml extra virgin olive oil
- Balsamic glaze, for drizzling
- Salt and pepper to taste
- Wooden skewers

Instruction:

1. Thread the cherry tomatoes, fresh mozzarella cheese, and fresh basil leaves alternately onto the wooden skewers, creating Caprese skewers.
2. Place the skewers in Zone 1 of the Ninja Dual Zone Air Fryer, ensuring they are arranged in a single layer.
3. Select Zone 1, choose the AIR FRY program, and set the temperature to 180°C. Set the time to 5 minutes.
4. Press the START/STOP button to begin cooking.
5. After 2 minutes of cooking, carefully open the air fryer and flip the skewers for even cooking.
6. Continue cooking for the remaining 3 minutes or until the cheese is slightly melted and the tomatoes are softened.
7. Once cooked, remove the skewers from the air fryer and let them cool slightly.
8. Drizzle the Caprese skewers with extra virgin olive oil and balsamic glaze.
9. Season with salt and pepper to taste.
10. Serve the **Caprese Skewers** as an appetizer or side dish.

Cheese Straws

Prep: **15** Min | Cook: **8** Min | Serves: **4**

Ingredient:

- 200g puff pastry, thawed
- 100g grated cheddar cheese
- 1 tsp paprika
- 1/2 tsp garlic powder
- Salt and pepper to taste
- 1 egg, beaten (for egg wash)

Instruction:

1. On a lightly floured surface, roll out the puff pastry to a thickness of about 3mm.
2. In a bowl, mix together the grated cheddar cheese, paprika, garlic powder, salt, and pepper.
3. Sprinkle the cheese mixture evenly over the puff pastry.
4. Gently press the cheese mixture into the pastry to ensure it sticks.
5. Cut the pastry into strips, approximately 1.5cm wide and 15cm long.
6. Twist each strip gently to create a spiral shape.
7. Place the twisted cheese straws in Zone 1 of the Ninja Dual Zone Air Fryer, ensuring they are arranged in a single layer.
8. Select Zone 1, choose the AIR FRY program, and set the temperature to 180°C. Set the time to 8 minutes.
9. Press the START/STOP button to begin cooking.
10. After 4 minutes of cooking, carefully open the air fryer and brush the cheese straws with the beaten egg wash.
11. Continue cooking for the remaining 4 minutes or until the cheese straws are golden brown and crispy.
12. Once cooked, remove the cheese straws from the air fryer and let them cool slightly.
13. Serve the **Cheese Straws** as a delightful snack or appetizer.

Chapter 06: Appetizers & Snacks

Chicken Satay Skewers

Prep: **20** Min | Cook: **10** Min | Serves: **4**

Ingredient:

- 400g boneless, skinless chicken breasts, cut into strips
- 3 tbsp smooth peanut butter
- 2 tbsp soy sauce
- 2 tbsp honey
- 2 tbsp lime juice
- 1 garlic clove, minced
- 1 tsp curry powder
- 1/2 tsp turmeric powder
- Salt and pepper to taste
- Wooden skewers, soaked in water for 30 minutes

Instruction:

1. In a bowl, whisk together the peanut butter, soy sauce, honey, lime juice, minced garlic, curry powder, turmeric powder, salt, and pepper to make the satay marinade.
2. Add the chicken strips to the marinade, making sure they are well-coated. Allow them to marinate for at least 10 minutes.
3. Thread the marinated chicken strips onto the soaked wooden skewers.
4. Place the skewers in Zone 1 of the Ninja Dual Zone Air Fryer, ensuring they are arranged in a single layer.
5. Select Zone 1, choose the AIR FRY program, and set the temperature to 200°C. Set the time to 10 minutes.
6. Press the START/STOP button to begin cooking.
7. After 5 minutes of cooking, carefully open the air fryer and flip the skewers for even cooking.
8. Continue cooking for the remaining 5 minutes or until the chicken is cooked through and slightly charred.
9. Once cooked, remove the chicken satay skewers from the air fryer and let them cool slightly.
10. Serve the **Chicken Satay Skewers** with a side of peanut sauce or your favorite dipping sauce.

Crackers and Cheese

Prep: **5** Min | Cook: **5** Min | Serves: **4**

Ingredient:

- 200g crackers (such as water biscuits or cream crackers)
- 200g cheddar cheese, sliced
- 20g butter, melted
- 1 tsp dried herbs (such as thyme or oregano)

Instruction:

1. Place the crackers in Zone 1 of the Ninja Dual Zone Air Fryer, ensuring they are arranged in a single layer.
2. Select Zone 1, choose the AIR FRY program, and set the temperature to 180°C. Set the time to 5 minutes.
3. Press the START/STOP button to begin cooking.
4. While the crackers are cooking, brush the sliced cheddar cheese with melted butter on both sides.
5. After 3 minutes of cooking, carefully open the air fryer and place the buttered cheese slices on top of the partially cooked crackers.
6. Sprinkle the dried herbs over the cheese and crackers.
7. Continue cooking for the remaining 2 minutes or until the cheese is melted and bubbly, and the crackers are golden brown.
8. Once cooked, remove the Crackers and Cheese from the air fryer and let them cool slightly.
9. Serve the **Crackers and Cheese** as a tasty snack or appetizer.

Chapter 06: Appetizers & Snacks

Crispy Calamari

Prep: **15** Min | Cook: **8** Min | Serves: **4**

Ingredient:

- 400g calamari rings
- 100g all-purpose flour
- 50g cornstarch
- 1 tsp paprika
- 1/2 tsp garlic powder
- Salt and pepper to taste
- 1 egg, beaten
- Lemon wedges, for serving
- Tartar sauce or aioli, for dipping

Instruction:

1. In a bowl, combine the all-purpose flour, cornstarch, paprika, garlic powder, salt, and pepper to create the coating mixture.
2. Dip each calamari ring into the beaten egg, then coat it with the flour mixture, shaking off any excess.
3. Place the coated calamari rings in Zone 1 and Zone 2 of the Ninja Dual Zone Air Fryer, ensuring they are arranged in a single layer.
4. Select Zone 1, choose the AIR FRY program, and set the temperature to 200°C. Set the time to 8 minutes. Select MATCH.
5. Press the START/STOP button to begin cooking.
6. After 4 minutes of cooking, carefully open the air fryer and shake the basket to ensure even cooking.
7. Continue cooking for the remaining 4 minutes or until the calamari rings are golden brown and crispy.
8. Once cooked, remove the Crispy Calamari from the air fryer and let them cool slightly.
9. Serve the **Crispy Calamari** with lemon wedges and your choice of tartar sauce or aioli for dipping.

Falafel

Prep: **20** Min | Cook: **12** Min | Serves: **4**

Ingredient:

- 400g canned chickpeas, drained and rinsed
- 1 small onion, roughly chopped
- 2 garlic cloves, minced
- 2 tbsp fresh parsley, chopped
- 2 tbsp fresh coriander, chopped
- 1 tsp ground cumin
- 1 tsp ground coriander
- 1/2 tsp baking powder
- 2 tbsp all-purpose flour
- Salt and pepper to taste
- Olive oil, for brushing

Instruction:

1. In a food processor, combine the drained and rinsed chickpeas, chopped onion, minced garlic, fresh parsley, fresh coriander, ground cumin, ground coriander, baking powder, all-purpose flour, salt, and pepper. Pulse until the mixture forms a coarse paste.
2. Shape the mixture into small falafel balls, about 3cm in diameter.
3. Place the falafel balls in Zone 1 and Zone 2 of the Ninja Dual Zone Air Fryer, ensuring they are arranged in a single layer.
4. Select Zone 1, choose the AIR FRY program, and set the temperature to 200°C. Set the time to 12 minutes. Select MATCH.
5. Press the START/STOP button to begin cooking.
6. After 6 minutes of cooking, carefully open the air fryer and brush the falafel balls with a little olive oil.
7. Continue cooking for the remaining 6 minutes or until the falafel balls are golden brown and crispy.
8. Once cooked, remove the Falafel from the air fryer and let them cool slightly.
9. Serve the **Falafel** as a delicious appetizer or in pita bread with your choice of toppings and sauces.

Chapter 06: Appetizers & Snacks

Garlic Bread

Prep: **10** Min | Cook: **8** Min | Serves: **4**

Ingredient:

- 4 slices of bread (white or crusty bread)
- 50g unsalted butter, softened
- 2 garlic cloves, minced
- 1 tbsp fresh parsley, chopped
- Salt to taste

Instruction:

1. In a small bowl, combine the softened butter, minced garlic, chopped parsley, and salt to make the garlic butter spread.
2. Spread the garlic butter mixture evenly on one side of each bread slice.
3. Place the bread slices, buttered side up, in Zone 1 of the Ninja Dual Zone Air Fryer.
4. Select Zone 1, choose the AIR FRY program, and set the temperature to 180°C. Set the time to 8 minutes.
5. Press the START/STOP button to begin cooking.
6. After 4 minutes of cooking, carefully open the air fryer and flip the bread slices for even cooking.
7. Continue cooking for the remaining 4 minutes or until the garlic bread is golden brown and crispy.
8. Once cooked, remove the Garlic Bread from the air fryer and let it cool slightly.
9. Serve the **Garlic Bread** as a delicious side dish or with your favorite pasta or soup.

Garlic Parmesan Knots

Prep: 15 Min | Cook: 10 Min | Serves: 4

Ingredient:

- 250g pizza dough (store-bought or homemade)
- 2 tbsp unsalted butter, melted
- 2 cloves garlic, minced
- 2 tbsp fresh parsley, chopped
- 30g grated Parmesan cheese
- Salt to taste

Instruction:

1. On a lightly floured surface, roll out the pizza dough into a rectangle, about 30cm x 20cm.
2. Cut the dough into strips, about 2cm wide.
3. Take each strip and tie it into a knot, tucking the ends underneath. Repeat with all the strips.
4. In a small bowl, combine the melted butter, minced garlic, chopped parsley, grated Parmesan cheese, and salt.
5. Dip each knot into the garlic butter mixture, ensuring they are coated evenly.
6. Place the garlic knots in Zone 1 of the Ninja Dual Zone Air Fryer, ensuring they are arranged in a single layer.
7. Select Zone 1, choose the AIR FRY program, and set the temperature to 180°C for 10 minutes. Press the START/STOP.
8. After 5 minutes of cooking, carefully open the air fryer and brush the garlic knots with any remaining garlic butter mixture.
9. Continue cooking for the remaining 5 minutes or until the garlic knots are golden brown and cooked through.
10. Once cooked, remove the Garlic Parmesan Knots from the air fryer and let them cool slightly.
11. Serve the **Garlic Parmesan Knots** as a delicious appetizer or as a side to pasta dishes or soups.

Chapter 06: Appetizers & Snacks

Halloumi Fries

Prep: 10 Min | Cook: 10 Min | Serves: 4

Ingredient:

- 250g halloumi cheese
- 60g all-purpose flour
- 1 tsp smoked paprika
- 1/2 tsp garlic powder
- Salt and pepper to taste
- 2 eggs, beaten
- Olive oil spray

Instruction:

1. Cut the halloumi cheese into fries, about 1cm thick and 8cm long.
2. In a shallow bowl, combine the all-purpose flour, smoked paprika, garlic powder, salt, and pepper.
3. Dip each halloumi fry into the beaten eggs, then coat it with the flour mixture, shaking off any excess.
4. Place the coated halloumi fries in Zone 1 of the Ninja Dual Zone Air Fryer, ensuring they are arranged in a single layer.
5. Select Zone 1, choose the AIR FRY program, and set the temperature to 200°C. Set the time to 10 minutes.
6. Press the START/STOP button to begin cooking.
7. After 5 minutes of cooking, carefully open the air fryer and spray the halloumi fries with olive oil.
8. Continue cooking for the remaining 5 minutes or until the halloumi fries are golden brown and crispy.
9. Once cooked, remove the Halloumi Fries from the air fryer and let them cool slightly.
10. Serve the **Halloumi Fries** as a delicious appetizer or snack, accompanied by a dipping sauce of your choice.

Jalapeno Poppers

Prep: **20** Min | Cook: **10** Min | Serves: **4**

Ingredient:

- 8 large jalapeno peppers
- 100g cream cheese, softened
- 50g cheddar cheese, grated
- 1/2 tsp garlic powder
- 1/4 tsp smoked paprika
- Salt and pepper to taste
- 60g all-purpose flour
- 2 eggs, beaten
- 80g breadcrumbs
- Olive oil spray

Instruction:

1. Cut each jalapeno pepper in half lengthwise and remove the seeds and membranes.
2. In a mixing bowl, combine the softened cream cheese, grated cheddar cheese, garlic powder, smoked paprika, salt, and pepper. Mix until well combined. Spoon the cheese mixture into each jalapeno half, filling them evenly.
3. Place the all-purpose flour in one shallow bowl, beaten eggs in another bowl, and breadcrumbs in a third bowl.
4. Dip each stuffed jalapeno half into the flour, then into the beaten eggs, and finally coat it with breadcrumbs. Ensure they are coated evenly.
5. Place the coated jalapeno poppers in Zone 1 and Zone 2 of the Ninja Dual Zone Air Fryer.
6. Select Zone 1, choose the AIR FRY program, and set the temperature to 200°C for 10 minutes. Select MATCH. Press the START/STOP button to begin cooking.
7. After 5 minutes of cooking, carefully open the air fryer and spray the jalapeno poppers with olive oil. Continue cooking for the remaining 5 minutes.
8. Serve the **Jalapeno Poppers** as a delicious appetizer or party snack, and enjoy!

Chapter 06: Appetizers & Snacks

Mini Meatballs

Prep: **15** Min | Cook: **12** Min | Serves: **4**

Ingredient:

- 300g minced beef
- 1 small onion, finely chopped
- 1 garlic clove, minced
- 20g breadcrumbs
- 1 egg, beaten
- 2 tbsp fresh parsley, chopped
- 1/2 tsp dried oregano
- Salt and pepper to taste
- Olive oil spray

Instruction:

1. In a mixing bowl, combine the minced beef, finely chopped onion, minced garlic, breadcrumbs, beaten egg, chopped parsley, dried oregano, salt, and pepper. Mix until well combined.
2. Shape the mixture into small meatballs, about 2cm in diameter.
3. Place the meatballs in Zone 1 and Zone 2 of the Ninja Dual Zone Air Fryer, ensuring they are arranged in a single layer.
4. Select Zone 1, choose the AIR FRY program, and set the temperature to 200°C. Set the time to 12 minutes. Select MATCH.
5. Press the START/STOP button to begin cooking.
6. After 6 minutes of cooking, carefully open the air fryer and shake the basket or use tongs to turn the meatballs for even cooking.
7. Spray the meatballs with olive oil.
8. Continue cooking for the remaining 6 minutes or until the meatballs are browned and cooked through.
9. Once cooked, remove the Mini Meatballs from the air fryer and let them cool slightly.
10. Serve the **Mini Meatballs** as a tasty appetizer, or with pasta, rice, or as a sandwich filling.

Mini Quiches

Prep: **20** Min | Cook: **12** Min | Serves: **4**

Ingredient:

- 150g shortcrust pastry
- 3 large eggs
- 80ml milk
- 50g cheddar cheese, grated
- 50g cooked ham, diced
- 1/4 red bell pepper, finely chopped
- 1/4 onion, finely chopped
- Salt and pepper to taste
- Olive oil spray

Instruction:

1. Roll out the shortcrust pastry on a lightly floured surface until it is about 2-3mm thick. Using a round cookie cutter or a glass, cut out circles from the pastry to fit your mini quiche molds.
2. Lightly grease the mini quiche molds with olive oil spray.
3. Press each pastry circle into the molds, ensuring they cover the bottom and sides.
4. In a mixing bowl, whisk together the eggs and milk until well combined. Add the grated cheddar cheese, diced ham, finely chopped red bell pepper, finely chopped onion, salt, and pepper to the egg mixture. Stir to combine.
5. Pour the egg mixture into each pastry-lined mold, filling them about 3/4 full.
6. Place the mini quiches in Zone 1 of the Ninja Dual Zone Air Fryer, ensuring they are arranged in a single layer.
7. Select Zone 1, choose the AIR FRY program, and set the temperature to 180°C for 12 minutes. Press the START/STOP.
8. After 6 minutes of cooking, carefully open the air fryer and rotate the quiche molds for even cooking. Continue cooking for the remaining 6 minutes.
9. Serve the **Mini Quiches** as a delightful appetizer or as part of a brunch spread.

Chapter 06: Appetizers & Snacks

Mozzarella Sticks

Prep: **20** Min | Cook: **8** Min | Serves: **4**

Ingredient:

- 200g mozzarella cheese, cut into sticks
- 100g plain flour
- 2 eggs, beaten
- 100g breadcrumbs
- 1/2 tsp dried oregano
- 1/2 tsp garlic powder
- Salt and pepper to taste
- Olive oil spray

Instruction:

1. In a shallow bowl, combine the plain flour with a pinch of salt and pepper. In another shallow bowl, whisk together the beaten eggs. In a third shallow bowl, mix the breadcrumbs with dried oregano, garlic powder, salt, and pepper.
2. Dip each mozzarella stick into the flour mixture, shaking off any excess. Then, dip it into the beaten eggs, allowing any excess to drip off. Finally, coat it in the breadcrumb mixture, pressing gently to adhere the breadcrumbs to the surface. Repeat with the remaining mozzarella sticks.
3. Place the coated mozzarella sticks in Zone 1 of the Ninja Dual Zone Air Fryer, ensuring they are arranged in a single layer.
4. Select Zone 1, choose the AIR FRY program, and set the temperature to 200°C. Set the time to 8 minutes.
5. Press the START/STOP button to begin cooking.
6. After 4 minutes of cooking, carefully open the air fryer and shake the basket or use tongs to turn the mozzarella sticks for even cooking.
7. Continue cooking for the remaining 4 minutes or until the mozzarella sticks are golden brown and crispy, and the cheese is melted inside.
8. Once cooked, remove the Mozzarella Sticks from the air fryer and let them cool slightly.
9. Serve the **Mozzarella Sticks** as a delicious appetizer or snack, with marinara sauce or any dipping sauce of your choice.

Onion Rings

Prep: **15** Min | Cook: **12** Min | Serves: **4**

Ingredient:

- 2 large onions, peeled and cut into rings
- 100g plain flour
- 1/2 tsp paprika
- 1/2 tsp garlic powder
- 1/4 tsp cayenne pepper (optional, for a bit of heat)
- Salt and pepper to taste
- 2 eggs, beaten
- 100g breadcrumbs
- Olive oil spray

Instruction:

1. In a shallow bowl, combine the plain flour with paprika, garlic powder, cayenne pepper (if using), salt, and pepper. In another shallow bowl, place the beaten eggs. In a third shallow bowl, place the breadcrumbs.
2. Dip each onion ring into the flour mixture, shaking off any excess. Then, dip it into the beaten eggs, allowing any excess to drip off. Finally, coat it in the breadcrumbs, pressing gently to adhere the breadcrumbs to the surface.
3. Place the coated onion rings in Zone 1 and Zone 2 of the Ninja Dual Zone Air Fryer, ensuring they are arranged in a single layer.
4. Select Zone 1, choose the AIR FRY program, and set the temperature to 200°C. Set the time to 12 minutes. Select MATCH.
5. Press the START/STOP button to begin cooking.
6. After 6 minutes of cooking, carefully open the air fryer and shake the basket or use tongs to flip the onion rings for even cooking.
7. Continue cooking for the remaining 6 minutes or until the onion rings are golden brown and crispy.
8. Once cooked, remove the Onion Rings from the air fryer and let them cool slightly.
9. Serve the **Onion Rings** as a delicious appetizer or side dish, with ketchup, mayo, or your favorite dipping sauce.

Chapter 06: Appetizers & Snacks

Pizza Bites

Prep: **15** Min | Cook: **10** Min | Serves: **4**

Ingredient:

- 200g pizza dough, store-bought or homemade
- 100g pizza sauce
- 100g mozzarella cheese, shredded
- 30g pepperoni slices, chopped
- 1/2 tsp dried oregano
- Olive oil spray

Instruction:

1. Roll out the pizza dough on a lightly floured surface to a thickness of about 1/2 cm. Cut the dough into small squares, about 3 cm each.
2. Place a small spoonful of pizza sauce onto each dough square. Top with shredded mozzarella cheese and chopped pepperoni. Sprinkle with dried oregano.
3. Fold the dough squares over the toppings to form small pockets, sealing the edges with your fingers. Repeat with the remaining dough and toppings.
4. Place the pizza bites in Zone 1 of the Ninja Dual Zone Air Fryer, ensuring they are arranged in a single layer.
5. Select Zone 1, choose the AIR FRY program, and set the temperature to 200°C. Set the time to 10 minutes.
6. Press the START/STOP button to begin cooking.
7. After 5 minutes of cooking, carefully open the air fryer and shake the basket or use tongs to turn the pizza bites for even cooking.
8. Continue cooking for the remaining 5 minutes or until the pizza bites are golden brown and the cheese is melted.
9. Once cooked, remove the Pizza Bites from the air fryer and let them cool slightly.
10. Serve the **Pizza Bites** as a delicious appetizer or snack, accompanied by additional pizza sauce for dipping.

Potato Skins

Prep: **15** Min | Cook: **25** Min | Serves: **4**

Ingredient:

- 4 medium-sized potatoes
- 2 tbsp olive oil
- 100g grated cheddar cheese
- 4 slices of bacon, cooked and crumbled
- 2 spring onions, finely chopped
- Salt and pepper to taste
- Sour cream (optional, for serving)

Instruction:

1. Wash the potatoes thoroughly and pat them dry. Using a fork, prick the potatoes several times.
2. Place the potatoes in Zone 1 of the Ninja Dual Zone Air Fryer, ensuring they are arranged in a single layer.
3. Select Zone 1, choose the AIR FRY program, and set the temperature to 200°C for 25 minutes. Press the START/STOP
4. After 15 minutes of cooking, open the air fryer and turn the potatoes. Continue cooking for the remaining 10 minutes.
5. Cut the potatoes in half lengthwise. Scoop out the flesh, leaving a thin layer of potato attached to the skins. Brush the potato skins with olive oil, both inside and outside. Season with salt and pepper.
6. Place the potato skins back in Zone 1 of the Ninja Dual Zone Air Fryer, ensuring they are arranged in a single layer.
7. Select Zone 1, choose the AIR FRY program, and set the temperature to 200°C for 5 minutes. Press the START/STOP.
8. After 2 minutes of cooking, carefully open the air fryer and sprinkle grated cheddar cheese, crumbled bacon, and chopped spring onions onto each potato skin. Continue cooking for the remaining 3 minutes or until the cheese is melted and bubbly.
9. Serve the **Potato Skins** as a delicious appetizer or side dish. Optionally, serve with sour cream on the side.

Chapter 06: Appetizers & Snacks

Samosas

Prep: **30** Min | Cook: **12** Min | Serves: **4**

Ingredient:

For the dough:
- 200g plain flour
- 1/2 tsp salt
- 2 tbsp vegetable oil
- 100-120ml water

For the filling:
- 2 medium potatoes, boiled and mashed
- 100g frozen peas, thawed
- 1 small onion, finely chopped
- 2 cloves garlic, minced
- 1 tsp grated ginger
- 1/2 tsp ground cumin
- 1/2 tsp ground coriander
- 1/2 tsp garam masala
- 1/4 tsp turmeric powder
- 1/4 tsp red chili powder (adjust to taste)
- Salt to taste
- 2 tbsp vegetable oil

Instruction:

1. In a large mixing bowl, combine the plain flour and salt. Add the vegetable oil and mix well. Gradually add water, a little at a time, and knead the mixture into a smooth and firm dough. Cover the dough with a damp cloth and let it rest for 15 minutes.
2. Meanwhile, prepare the filling. Heat 2 tablespoons of vegetable oil in a pan over medium heat. Add the chopped onion, minced garlic, and grated ginger. Sauté until the onion turns translucent.
3. Add the ground cumin, ground coriander, garam masala, turmeric powder, red chili powder, and salt. Stir well to combine the spices. Add the thawed peas and mashed potatoes to the pan. Cook for a few minutes, then remove from heat.
4. Divide the rested dough into small balls, about 2 cm in diameter. Roll out each ball into a thin circle, about 10 cm in diameter. Cut each rolled-out circle in half to form two semicircles.
5. Take one semicircle, fold it into a cone shape, and seal the edges using a little water. Fill the cone with a spoonful of the prepared filling. Seal the top edge of the cone by pressing it together.
6. Place the samosas in Zone 1 of the Ninja Dual Zone Air Fryer.
7. Select Zone 1, choose the AIR FRY program, and set the temperature to 180°C for 12 minutes. Press the START/STOP.
8. After 6 minutes of cooking, open the air fryer and flip the samosas for even cooking. Continue cooking for the remaining 6 minutes.
9. Serve the **Samosas** as a tasty appetizer or snack, accompanied by chutney or sauce of your choice.

Spring Rolls

Prep: **30** Min | Cook: **15** Min
Serves: **12 spring rolls**

Ingredient:

- 200g cooked chicken breast, shredded
- 100g cooked prawns, chopped
- 50g bean sprouts
- 1 teaspoon sesame oil
- 1/2 teaspoon sugar
- 50g carrots, julienned
- 50g cabbage, finely shredded
- 2 spring onions, finely chopped
- 2 cloves of garlic, minced
- 1 tablespoon soy sauce
- 1 tablespoon oyster sauce
- 1/4 teaspoon black pepper
- 12 spring roll wrappers
- 1 tablespoon cornstarch mixed with 2 tablespoons water (for sealing)
- Cooking oil spray

Instruction:

1. In a bowl, combine the shredded chicken breast, chopped prawns, bean sprouts, carrots, cabbage, spring onions, minced garlic, soy sauce, oyster sauce, sesame oil, sugar, and black pepper. Mix well to combine. Lay a spring roll wrapper on a clean surface, with one corner pointing towards you. Place about 2 tablespoons of the filling mixture in the center of the wrapper.
2. Fold the bottom corner of the wrapper over the filling and tuck it tightly. Fold the left and right corners towards the center.
3. Gently roll the wrapper from the bottom towards the top, ensuring the filling is tightly wrapped. Use the cornstarch and water mixture to seal the edge of the wrapper. Repeat the process with the remaining spring roll wrappers and filling.
4. Evenly dividing spring rolls between the two zone in a single layer, leaving space between them.
5. Select Zone 1, choose the AIR FRY program, and set the temperature to 180°C. Set the time to 15 minutes. Select MATCH. Press the START/STOP button to begin cooking.
6. After 7 minutes, lightly spray the spring rolls with cooking oil spray.
7. Carefully remove the air fryer basket and transfer the cooked spring rolls to a serving plate. Serve the **Spring Rolls** hot with your favorite dipping sauce, such as sweet chili sauce or soy sauce.

Chapter 06: Appetizers & Snacks

Stuffed Potato Bites

Prep: **15** Min | Cook: **20** Min | Serves: **4**

Ingredient:

- 500g potatoes, peeled and diced into small cubes
- 100g cheddar cheese, grated
- 50g cooked bacon, crumbled
- 2 tablespoons chopped fresh chives
- 1/4 teaspoon garlic powder
- 1/4 teaspoon onion powder
- 1/4 teaspoon salt
- 1/4 teaspoon black pepper
- Cooking oil spray

Instruction:

1. Place the diced potatoes in a microwave-safe bowl and cover with a microwave-safe plate. Microwave on high for 5-6 minutes, or until the potatoes are fork-tender.
2. In a mixing bowl, combine the cooked potatoes, grated cheddar cheese, crumbled bacon, chopped fresh chives, garlic powder, onion powder, salt, and black pepper. Mix well to combine.
3. In Zone 1, scoop tablespoon-sized portions of the potato mixture and shape them into small round bites. Place the stuffed potato bites in a single layer, leaving space between them.
4. Select Zone 1, choose the AIR FRY program, and set the temperature to 200°C. Set the time to 20 minutes.
5. Press the START/STOP button to begin cooking.
6. After 10 minutes of air frying in Zone 1, carefully remove the air fryer basket and lightly spray the stuffed potato bites with cooking oil spray. Return the basket to the air fryer.
7. Continue cooking for the remaining 10 minutes or until the potato bites are golden brown and crispy.
8. Carefully remove the air fryer basket and transfer the cooked stuffed potato bites to a serving plate.
9. Serve the **Stuffed Potato Bites** hot as a delicious appetizer or snack.

Tempura Vegetables

Prep: **15** Min | Cook: **10** Min | Serves: **4**

Ingredient:

- 200g plain flour
- 2 tablespoons cornstarch
- 1/2 teaspoon baking powder
- 1/2 teaspoon salt
- 200ml ice-cold sparkling water
- Assorted vegetables (such as bell peppers, zucchini, broccoli, and mushrooms), cut into bite-sized pieces
- Cooking oil spray
- Dipping sauce (such as soy sauce or tempura dipping sauce)

Instruction:

1. In a mixing bowl, combine the plain flour, cornstarch, baking powder, and salt. Mix well.
2. Gradually pour in the ice-cold sparkling water while whisking the mixture. Continue whisking until the batter is smooth and free of lumps.
3. In Zone 1, place the assorted vegetable pieces in a single layer, leaving space between them.
4. Select Zone 1, choose the AIR FRY program, and set the temperature to 200°C. Set the time to 10 minutes.
5. Press the START/STOP button to begin cooking.
6. After 5 minutes of air frying in Zone 1, carefully remove the air fryer basket and lightly spray the vegetables with cooking oil spray. Return the basket to the air fryer.
7. Continue cooking for the remaining 5 minutes or until the vegetables are crispy and golden brown.
8. Carefully remove the air fryer basket and transfer the cooked tempura vegetables to a serving plate.
9. Serve the **Tempura Vegetables** hot with your choice of dipping sauce.

Chapter 06: Appetizers & Snacks

Yorkshire Puddings

Prep: **10** Min | Cook: **20** Min | Serves: **4**

Ingredient:

- 100g plain flour
- 1/4 teaspoon salt
- 2 large eggs
- 200ml milk
- Vegetable oil or beef dripping, for greasing

Instruction:

1. In a mixing bowl, combine the plain flour and salt. Make a well in the center.
2. Crack the eggs into the well and gradually whisk them into the flour, incorporating a little flour at a time.
3. Slowly pour in the milk while whisking the mixture. Continue whisking until the batter is smooth and free of lumps. Let the batter rest for 30 minutes at room temperature.
4. In Zone 1, evenly distribute a small amount of vegetable oil or beef dripping into each well of a Yorkshire pudding tin or a muffin tray.
5. Place the tin/tray to Zone 1 and select Zone 1. Choose the AIR FRY program and set the temperature to 220°C. Set the time to 20 minutes.
6. Press the START/STOP button to begin cooking.
7. Avoid opening the air fryer during cooking to prevent the Yorkshire puddings from deflating. After 20 minutes, check if the Yorkshire puddings are risen, golden brown, and crispy.
8. Carefully remove the tin/tray from the air fryer and transfer the Yorkshire puddings to a serving plate.
9. Serve the **Yorkshire Puddings** immediately as a side dish for roast beef or as a part of a traditional Sunday roast.

Blueberry Scones

Prep: **15** Min | Cook: **12** Min | Serves: **6 scones**

Ingredient:

- 225g self-raising flour
- 50g unsalted butter, cold and cubed
- 25g caster sugar
- 100g fresh blueberries
- 120ml milk
- 1/2 teaspoon vanilla extract
- Clotted cream and strawberry jam, to serve

Instruction:

1. In a mixing bowl, combine the self-raising flour and cold, cubed unsalted butter. Rub the butter into the flour using your fingertips until the mixture resembles breadcrumbs.
2. Stir in the caster sugar and fresh blueberries. Make a well in the center of the mixture. Pour in the milk and vanilla extract. Mix the ingredients together with a spoon until they form a soft dough.
3. Turn the dough out onto a lightly floured surface and gently knead it a few times until it comes together.
4. Shape the dough into a circle about 2cm thick. Use a round cutter to cut out individual scones from the dough. Evenly dividing scones between the two zone in a single layer.
5. Select Zone 1, choose the BAKE program, and set the temperature to 180°C. Set the time to 12 minutes. Select MATCH. Press the START/STOP button to begin cooking.
6. After 6 minutes, carefully remove the air fryer basket and lightly brush the tops of the scones with milk. Return the basket to the air fryer and continue cooking for the remaining 6 minutes or until the scones are golden brown and cooked through.
7. Carefully remove the air fryer basket and transfer the cooked blueberry scones to a wire rack to cool slightly.
8. Serve the **Blueberry Scones** warm with clotted cream and strawberry jam.

Chapter 07: Desserts

Bread Pudding

Prep: **15** Min | Cook: **30** Min | Serves: **4**

Ingredient:

- 300g stale bread, torn into small pieces
- 500ml whole milk
- 100g granulated sugar
- 2 large eggs
- 1 teaspoon vanilla extract
- 1/2 teaspoon ground cinnamon
- 50g raisins or sultanas
- Butter, for greasing the baking dish
- Demerara sugar, for sprinkling on top

Instruction:

1. In a large mixing bowl, combine the torn stale bread, whole milk, and granulated sugar. Let the mixture sit for about 10 minutes, stirring occasionally, until the bread has absorbed the milk.
2. In a separate bowl, beat the eggs with the vanilla extract and ground cinnamon.
3. Pour the beaten egg mixture over the soaked bread mixture and stir well to combine.
4. Stir in the raisins or sultanas.
5. Grease a baking dish with butter and transfer the bread pudding mixture into the dish, spreading it out evenly.
6. Sprinkle demerara sugar on top of the bread pudding.
7. In Zone 1, place the baking dish in a single layer.
8. Select Zone 1, choose the AIR FRY program, and set the temperature to 180°C. Set the time to 30 minutes.
9. Press the START/STOP button to begin cooking.
10. After 15 minutes of air frying in Zone 1, carefully remove the baking dish from the air fryer and cover it loosely with aluminum foil to prevent the top from browning too much.
11. Return the baking dish to Zone 1 and continue cooking for the remaining 15 minutes.
12. Carefully remove the baking dish from the air fryer and let the bread pudding cool slightly before serving. Serve the **Bread Pudding** warm as is or with custard or vanilla ice cream, if desired.

Cherry Bakewell Tarts

Prep: **30** Min | Cook: **15** Min | Serves: **6 tarts**

Ingredient:

For the pastry:
- 200g plain flour
- 100g unsalted butter, chilled and cubed
- 50g icing sugar
- 1 large egg yolk
- 1-2 tablespoons cold water

For the filling:
- 150g cherry jam
- 150g ground almonds
- 100g unsalted butter, softened
- 100g caster sugar
- 2 large eggs
- 1/2 teaspoon almond extract

For the topping:
- 50g flaked almonds
- Icing sugar, for dusting

Instruction:

1. In a mixing bowl, combine the plain flour, chilled and cubed unsalted butter, and icing sugar. Rub the butter into the flour until it resembles breadcrumbs.
2. Add the egg yolk and 1 tbsp cold water. Stir until a dough forms.
3. Turn out the dough onto a floured surface and gently knead. Wrap the dough in cling film and refrigerate for 15 minutes.
4. Roll out the dough to about 3mm thickness. Use a round cutter to cut out circles slightly larger than the tart tin holes. Press the pastry circles into the tart tin holes to cover the base and sides.
5. In a mixing bowl, beat the butter and sugar until light and fluffy. Gradually add the eggs, beating well after each addition. Stir in the ground almonds and almond extract.
6. Spoon 1 tsp cherry jam into the center of each pastry case.
7. Spoon the almond mixture over the jam, filling almost to the top.
8. In Zone 1, place the tart tin in a single layer. Select Zone 1, choose the BAKE program, and set the temperature to 180°C. Set the time to 15 minutes. Press the START/STOP.
9. After 10, sprinkle the flaked almonds over the top of each tart. Allow the tarts to cool in the tin for a few minutes before transferring them to a wire rack to cool completely.
10. Dust the **Cherry Bakewell Tarts** with icing sugar before serving.

Chapter 07: Desserts

Chocolate Chip Cookies

Prep: **15** Min | Cook: **12** Min | Serves: **18 cookies**

Ingredient:

- 150g unsalted butter, softened
- 150g light brown sugar
- 100g granulated sugar
- 1 large egg
- 1 teaspoon vanilla extract
- 250g plain flour
- 1/2 teaspoon baking soda
- 1/4 teaspoon salt
- 200g chocolate chips

Instruction:

1. In a large mixing bowl, cream together the softened butter, light brown sugar, and granulated sugar until light and fluffy.
2. Add the egg and vanilla extract to the mixture, and beat until well combined.
3. In a separate bowl, whisk together the plain flour, baking soda, and salt. Gradually add the dry ingredients to the wet ingredients, mixing until just combined.
4. Fold in the chocolate chips until evenly distributed throughout the cookie dough.
5. Divide the cookie dough into approximately 18 equal-sized portions and shape them into balls.
6. Evenly dividing cookie dough balls between the two zone, leaving some space between them for spreading.
7. Select Zone 1, choose the AIR FRY program, and set the temperature to 180°C. Set the time to 10-12 minutes to bake the cookies. Select MATCH. Press the START/STOP.
8. Halfway through the cooking time, pause the air fryer and gently flatten each cookie with a fork or the palm of your hand.
9. Resume cooking until the cookies are golden brown around the edges and slightly soft in the center.
10. Carefully remove the cookies from the air fryer and let them cool on a wire rack. Once cooled, serve and enjoy the delicious homemade **chocolate chip cookies**!

Cinnamon Rolls

Prep: **20** Min | Cook: **12** Min
Serves: **8 cinnamon rolls**

Ingredient:

For the dough:
- 300g plain flour
- 50g granulated sugar
- 1 teaspoon instant yeast
- 1/2 teaspoon salt
- 150ml warm milk
- 50g unsalted butter, melted
- 1 large egg

For the filling:
- 50g unsalted butter, softened
- 100g light brown sugar
- 2 teaspoons ground cinnamon

For the glaze:
- 100g icing sugar
- 2 tablespoons milk
- 1/2 teaspoon vanilla extract

Instruction:

1. In a mixing bowl, combine the plain flour, granulated sugar, instant yeast, and salt.
2. Whisk warm milk, melted unsalted butter, and egg in another bowl. Pour wet ingredients into dry ingredients and mix until dough forms. Turn the dough out onto a lightly floured surface and knead for about 5 minutes until the dough is smooth and elastic. Place dough in greased bowl, cover, and let rise for 1 hour until doubled. Roll out the risen dough into a rectangle with a thickness of about 0.5 cm.
3. In a small bowl, mix together the softened unsalted butter, light brown sugar, and ground cinnamon to make the filling. Spread the filling evenly over the rolled-out dough, leaving a small border around the edges. Starting from one of the long sides, tightly roll up the dough into a log. Cut the log into 8 equal slices.
4. Evenly dividing cinnamon roll slices between the two zone. Select Zone 1, choose the AIR FRY program, and set the temperature to 180°C. Set the time to 12 minutes. Select MATCH. Press the START/STOP button to begin cooking.
5. Cover with foil after 6 minutes. Let rolls cool slightly after cooking. In a small bowl, whisk together the icing sugar, milk, and vanilla extract to make the glaze.
6. Drizzle glaze over warm **cinnamon rolls**. Enjoy!

Chapter 07: Desserts

Coconut Macaroons

Prep: **15** Min | Cook: **15** Min
Serves: **12 macaroons**

Ingredient:

- 200g desiccated coconut
- 150g condensed milk
- 50g granulated sugar
- 2 large egg whites
- 1/2 teaspoon vanilla extract

Instruction:

1. In a mixing bowl, combine the desiccated coconut, condensed milk, granulated sugar, egg whites, and vanilla extract. Mix well until all the ingredients are thoroughly combined.
2. Scoop tablespoonfuls of the coconut mixture and shape them into compact mounds using your hands.
3. Place brownies evenly on 2 parchment-lined baking trays.
4. Place two baking trays in two zone.
5. Select Zone 1, choose the AIR FRY program, and set the temperature to 180°C. Set the time to 10 minutes. Select MATCH.
6. Press the START/STOP button to begin cooking.
7. After 5 minutes of air frying in Zone 1, carefully remove the baking sheet from the air fryer and lightly flatten the tops of the macaroons with the back of a spoon.
8. Return the baking sheet to Zone 1 and continue cooking for the remaining 5 minutes or until the macaroons are golden brown on the outside.
9. Carefully remove the baking sheet from the air fryer and allow the macaroons to cool on the baking sheet for a few minutes.
10. Transfer the macaroons to a wire rack to cool completely before serving.
11. Enjoy your delightful **Coconut Macaroons**!

Custard Tarts

Prep: **20** Min | Cook: **12** Min

Serves: **8 custard tarts**

Ingredient:

For the pastry:
- 200g plain flour
- 100g unsalted butter, cold and cubed
- 2 tablespoons granulated sugar
- 1 large egg yolk
- 1-2 tablespoons cold water

For the custard filling:
- 500ml whole milk
- 4 large egg yolks
- 100g granulated sugar
- 2 tablespoons cornstarch
- 1 teaspoon vanilla extract
- Ground nutmeg, for sprinkling

Instruction:

1. Combine plain flour, cold cubed unsalted butter, and granulated sugar in a mixing bowl. Rub butter into flour until mixture resembles breadcrumbs. Add egg yolk and mix well.
2. Turn dough onto lightly floured surface, knead gently until smooth. Refrigerate wrapped in plastic wrap for 30 minutes.
3. Roll out chilled pastry dough to 0,5cm thickness. Cut out 8 circles slightly larger than tart molds. Press pastry circles into greased tart molds, ensuring pastry comes up sides.
4. Heat whole milk in saucepan until hot but not boiling. Whisk together egg yolks, granulated sugar, cornstarch, and vanilla extract in separate bowl. Slowly pour hot milk into egg yolk mixture, whisking constantly.
5. Return mixture to saucepan, cook over medium heat, stirring continuously, until custard thickens. Remove custard from heat and let cool slightly. Pour custard into tart molds, filling about 3/4 full. Sprinkle ground nutmeg on each custard tart.
6. Evenly dividing tart molds between the two zone in single layer. Select Zone 1, choose the BAKE program, and set the temperature to 180°C. Set the time to 12 minutes. Select MATCH. Press the START/STOP.
7. After 6 minutes, cover tart molds loosely with foil. Let custard tarts cool in molds briefly. Enjoy your delightful **Custard Tarts**!

Chapter 07: Desserts

Lemon Drizzle Cakes

Prep: **15** Min | Cook: **12** Min

Serves: **6 mini lemon drizzle cakes**

Ingredient:

For the cakes:
- 175g unsalted butter, softened
- 175g caster sugar
- 3 large eggs
- 175g self-raising flour
- Zest of 2 lemons

For the lemon drizzle:
- Juice of 2 lemons
- 85g granulated sugar

For the icing (optional):
- 150g icing sugar
- Juice of 1 lemon

Instruction:

1. In a mixing bowl, cream together the softened unsalted butter and caster sugar until light and fluffy.
2. Beat in the eggs, one at a time, ensuring each egg is fully incorporated before adding the next one.
3. Sift the self-raising flour into the bowl and fold it into the batter until just combined. Be careful not to overmix.
4. Stir in the zest of 2 lemons to infuse the batter with lemon flavor.
5. Spoon the cake batter into greased and lined mini cake pans or silicone molds, filling them about two-thirds full.
6. In Zone 1, place the cake pans or molds in a single layer. Select Zone 1, choose the BAKE program, and set the temperature to 180°C. Set the time to 12 minutes. Press the START/STOP.
7. After 6 minutes, use a skewer to poke several holes in the tops of the cakes.
8. In a small bowl, mix together the juice of 2 lemons and granulated sugar to make the lemon drizzle.
9. Spoon the lemon drizzle evenly over the warm cakes, allowing it to soak into the holes and coat the tops.
10. Carefully remove the cake pans or molds from the air fryer and let the cakes cool in the pans or molds for a few minutes.
11. If desired, in a small bowl, whisk together the icing sugar and juice of 1 lemon to make the icing. Drizzle the icing over the cooled cakes. Enjoy your delicious **Lemon Drizzle Cakes**!

Mini Eclairs

Prep: **20** Min | Cook: **20** Min
Serves: **12 mini eclairs**

Ingredient:

For the choux pastry:
- 60g unsalted butter
- 125ml water
- 75g plain flour
- 2 large eggs

For the filling:
- 250ml double cream
- 1 tablespoon icing sugar
- 1 teaspoon vanilla extract

For the chocolate glaze:
- 100g dark chocolate, chopped
- 50g unsalted butter

Instruction:

1. In a saucepan, combine the unsalted butter and water. Heat until the butter has melted and the mixture boils. Remove from heat and add the plain flour. Stir until a smooth ball forms. Transfer the dough to a mixing bowl and let it cool. Add the eggs to the dough, one at a time, beating well after each addition. Transfer the dough to a piping bag fitted with a plain round tip.
2. Roll the dough into strips about 7cm long and divide evenly onto 2 baking trays lined with parchment paper.
3. Place two baking trays in two zone. Select Zone 1, choose the BAKE program, and set the temperature to 200°C. Set the time to 20 minutes. Select MATCH. Press the START/STOP.
4. After 10 minutes, carefully flip the eclairs over and continue cooking for the remaining 10 minutes.
5. Whip the double cream, icing sugar, and vanilla extract together until soft peaks form. Transfer the whipped cream to a piping bag fitted with a small round tip.
6. Once cooled, make a small slit in the side of each eclair. Pipe the whipped cream into the eclairs through the slit. In a microwave-safe bowl, combine the chopped dark chocolate and unsalted butter. Microwave until melted and smooth.
7. Dip the top of each eclair into the melted chocolate glaze.
8. Place the glazed **eclairs** on a wire rack to set.

Chapter 07: Desserts

Chelsea Buns

Prep: **25** Min | Cook: **15** Min
Serves: **12 Chelsea Buns**

Ingredient:

For the dough:
- 500g strong white bread flour
- 50g caster sugar
- 10g instant yeast
- 1 teaspoon salt
- 50g unsalted butter, melted
- 250ml milk, warmed
- 1 large egg, beaten

For the filling:
- 50g unsalted butter, softened
- 75g light brown sugar
- 2 teaspoons ground cinnamon
- 75g currants or raisins

For the glaze:
- 2 tablespoons apricot jam
- 1-2 tablespoons hot water

Instruction:

1. In a large mixing bowl, combine the bread flour, caster sugar, instant yeast, and salt. Make a well in the center and pour in the melted unsalted butter, warmed milk, and beaten egg.
2. Mix the ingredients together until a dough forms. Transfer the dough to a lightly floured surface and knead for about 10 minutes until smooth and elastic. Place the dough back into the bowl, cover with a clean kitchen towel, and let it rise in a warm place for about 1 hour or until doubled in size.
3. Roll out the dough into a rectangle approximately 30cm x 40cm.
4. Spread the softened unsalted butter evenly over the dough.
5. In a small bowl, mix together the light brown sugar and ground cinnamon. Sprinkle this mixture over the buttered dough.
6. Sprinkle the currants or raisins evenly over the dough.
7. Starting from the long edge, tightly roll up the dough into a log.
8. Using a sharp knife, cut the log into approximately 12 equal-sized slices. Evenly dividing slices between the two zone onto a baking sheet lined with parchment paper.
9. Select Zone 1, choose the BAKE program, and set the temperature to 180°C. Set the time to 12-15 minutes. Select MATCH. Press the START/STOP button to begin cooking.
10. In a small saucepan, heat the apricot jam and hot water together until melted and smooth. Remove the **Chelsea Buns** from the air fryer and brush them with the glaze while they are still warm.

Mixed Berry Crumbles

Prep: **15** Min | Cook: **20** Min | Serves: **4**

Ingredient:

For the filling:
- 400g mixed berries (such as strawberries, raspberries, blackberries, and blueberries)
- 50g caster sugar
- 1 tablespoon cornstarch
- 1 tablespoon lemon juice

For the crumble topping:
- 100g plain flour
- 50g unsalted butter, cold and cubed
- 50g rolled oats
- 50g demerara sugar

For serving:
- Whipped cream or vanilla ice cream (optional)

Instruction:

1. In a mixing bowl, combine the mixed berries, caster sugar, cornstarch, and lemon juice. Stir well to coat the berries evenly. Set aside.
2. In a separate bowl, combine the plain flour, cold unsalted butter cubes, rolled oats, and demerara sugar.
3. Use your fingertips to rub the butter into the dry ingredients until the mixture resembles coarse crumbs.
4. Divide the berry mixture evenly among four individual ramekins or oven-safe dishes.
5. In Zone 1, top each ramekin with the crumble mixture, evenly distributing it over the berries.
6. Select Zone 1, choose the BAKE program, and set the temperature to 180°C. Set the time to 15-20 minutes. Press the START/STOP button to begin cooking.
7. After 15-20 minutes of air frying in Zone 1, the crumbles should be golden brown and the berries bubbly.
8. Carefully remove the ramekins from the air fryer and let them cool for a few minutes.
9. Serve the **mixed berry crumbles** warm, optionally topped with whipped cream or vanilla ice cream.

Chapter 07: Desserts

Nutella-Stuffed Doughnuts

Prep: **25** Min | Cook: **10** Min
Serves: **2 doughnuts**

Ingredient:

- 275g plain flour
- 50g caster sugar
- 7g instant yeast
- 1/2 teaspoon salt
- 125ml warm milk
- 1 large egg, beaten
- 25g unsalted butter, melted
- Nutella or any chocolate-hazelnut spread, for filling
- Vegetable oil, for greasing

For the coating:
- 50g unsalted butter, melted
- 100g caster sugar

Instruction:

1. In a large mixing bowl, combine the plain flour, caster sugar, instant yeast, and salt. Make a well in the center and pour in the warm milk, beaten egg, and melted unsalted butter. Mix the ingredients together until a soft dough forms.
2. Transfer the dough to a lightly floured surface and knead for about 5 minutes until smooth and elastic.
3. Place the dough back into the bowl, cover with a clean kitchen towel, and let it rise in a warm place for about 1 hour or until doubled in size.
4. Eoll out the dough to a thickness of about 1cm. Use a round cookie cutter or a glass to cut out circles from the dough. Place a small amount of Nutella or chocolate-hazelnut spread in the center of each dough circle.
5. Fold the dough over the filling and pinch the edges to seal, forming a ball. Lightly grease the air fryer basket with vegetable oil to prevent sticking.
6. Evenly dividing stuffed doughnuts between the two zone, leaving space between each one. Select Zone 1, choose the AIR FRY program, and set the temperature to 180°C. Set the time to 8-10 minutes. Select MATCH. Press the START/STOP. Remove the doughnuts from the air fryer and let them cool slightly.
7. In a shallow bowl, combine the melted unsalted butter and caster sugar for the coating. Dip each **doughnut** into the melted butter, then roll it in the sugar mixture to coat.

Orange and Almond Cakes

Prep: **20** Min | Cook: **18** Min

Serves: **8 individual cakes**

Ingredient:

- 200g unsalted butter, softened
- 200g caster sugar
- 3 large eggs
- Zest of 2 oranges
- 200g self-raising flour
- 100g ground almonds
- 3 tablespoons freshly squeezed orange juice

For the glaze:
- Juice of 1 orange
- 50g icing sugar

Instruction:

1. In a mixing bowl, cream together the softened unsalted butter and caster sugar until light and fluffy. Add the eggs, one at a time, beating well after each addition. Stir in the orange zest.
2. Sift the self-raising flour into the bowl and fold it in gently.
3. Add the ground almonds and freshly squeezed orange juice to the mixture. Stir until well combined. Lightly grease individual silicone cupcake molds or ramekins with a little butter.
4. In Zone 1, divide the cake batter evenly among the molds or ramekins. Select Zone 1, choose the BAKE program, and set the temperature to 180°C. Set the time to 15-18 minutes.
5. Press the START/STOP button to begin cooking.
6. After 15-18 minutes, the cakes should be golden brown and cooked through. Use a toothpick to test for doneness.
7. Carefully remove the cakes from the air fryer and let them cool in the molds or ramekins for a few minutes.
8. In the meantime, prepare the glaze by combining the orange juice and icing sugar in a small bowl. Stir until smooth.
9. Once the cakes have cooled slightly, remove them from the molds or ramekins and place them on a wire rack.
10. Drizzle the glaze over the top of each cake, allowing it to drip down the sides. Enjoy your delicious **Orange and Almond Cakes**!

Chapter 07: Desserts

Peach Cobbler

Prep: **15** Min | Cook: **25** Min | Serves: **4-6**

Ingredient:

For the filling:
- 800g fresh or canned peaches, sliced
- 50g caster sugar
- 1 tablespoon cornstarch
- 1/2 teaspoon ground cinnamon
- Juice of 1/2 lemon

For the topping:
- 150g self-raising flour
- 50g caster sugar
- 75g unsalted butter, cold and cubed
- 100ml milk

For serving:
- Vanilla ice cream or whipped cream (optional)

Instruction:

1. In a mixing bowl, combine the sliced peaches, caster sugar, cornstarch, ground cinnamon, and lemon juice. Stir well to coat the peaches evenly. Set aside.
2. In a separate bowl, combine the self-raising flour and caster sugar.
3. Add the cold, cubed unsalted butter to the flour mixture. Use your fingertips to rub the butter into the flour until the mixture resembles coarse crumbs.
4. Gradually add the milk to the mixture, stirring until a soft dough forms.
5. Place the peach filling into an oven-safe dish or ramekins.
6. In Zone 1, drop spoonfuls of the dough topping evenly over the peaches.
7. Select Zone 1, choose the BAKE program, and set the temperature to 180°C. Set the time to 20-25 minutes.
8. Press the START/STOP button to begin cooking.
9. After 20-25 minutes of air frying in Zone 1, the peach cobbler should be golden brown and bubbling.
10. Carefully remove the dish or ramekins from the air fryer and let them cool for a few minutes.
11. Serve the **peach cobbler** warm, optionally topped with vanilla ice cream or whipped cream.

Pear and Almond Galettes

Prep: **20** Min | Cook: **18** Min | Serves: **4 galettes**

Ingredient:

For the pastry:
- 200g plain flour
- 100g unsalted butter, cold and cubed
- 1 tablespoon caster sugar
- 1/4 teaspoon salt
- 4-5 tablespoons cold water

For the filling:
- 2 ripe pears, thinly sliced
- 50g almond meal (ground almonds)
- 2 tablespoons caster sugar
- 1/2 teaspoon ground cinnamon
- 1 egg, beaten (for egg wash)

For serving:
- Icing sugar, for dusting
- Whipped cream or vanilla ice cream (optional)

Instruction:

1. In a mixing bowl, combine the plain flour, cold cubed unsalted butter, caster sugar, and salt. Use your fingertips to rub the butter into the flour mixture until it resembles breadcrumbs. Gradually add the cold water, one tablespoon at a time, and mix until the dough comes together. Be careful not to overmix.
2. Shape the dough into a ball, wrap it in plastic wrap, and refrigerate for 15 minutes. Divide the dough into 4 equal portions and roll each portion out into a circle about 15cm in diameter.
3. In Zone 1, place the rolled-out pastry circles in the air fryer basket.
4. In a small bowl, combine the almond meal, caster sugar, and ground cinnamon. Sprinkle the almond mixture evenly onto the center of each pastry circle, leaving a border around the edges. Arrange the thinly sliced pears over the almond mixture.
5. Fold the edges of the pastry over the filling, creating a rustic, free-form galette shape. Brush the edges of the pastry with the beaten egg wash.
6. Select Zone 1, choose the BAKE program, and set the temperature to 180°C. Set the time to 15-18 minutes. Press the START/STOP button to begin cooking.
7. Carefully remove the galettes from the air fryer and let them cool for a few minutes. Dust the **galettes** with icing sugar and serve warm. Optionally, top with whipped cream or vanilla ice cream.

Chapter 07: Desserts

Pineapple Upside-Down Cakes

Prep: **20** Min | Cook: **18** Min
Serves: **4 individual cakes**

Ingredient:

- 200g canned pineapple rings, drained
- 7-8 glacé cherries
- 150g unsalted butter, melted
- 150g caster sugar
- 2 large eggs
- 150g self-raising flour
- 1/2 teaspoon vanilla extract
- 2 tablespoons pineapple juice (from the canned pineapple rings)

Instruction:

1. Lightly grease four individual silicone cupcake molds or ramekins with a little butter.
2. In zone 1, place one pineapple ring in the bottom of each mold or ramekin. Place a glacé cherry in the center of each pineapple ring.
3. In a mixing bowl, cream together the melted unsalted butter and caster sugar until light and fluffy. Add the eggs, one at a time, beating well after each addition. Stir in the vanilla extract. Sift the self-raising flour into the bowl and fold it in gently.
4. Add the pineapple juice to the mixture and stir until well combined.
5. Divide the cake batter evenly among the molds or ramekins, pouring it over the pineapple and cherries.
6. In Zone 1, place the molds or ramekins in the air fryer basket.
7. Select Zone 1, choose the BAKE program, and set the temperature to 180°C. Set the time to 15-18 minutes. Press the START/STOP button to begin cooking.
8. After 15-18 minutes of air frying in Zone 1, the cakes should be golden brown and cooked through. Use a toothpick to test for doneness.
9. Invert each cake onto a serving plate, allowing the pineapple and cherries to be on top.
10. Serve the **pineapple upside-down cakes** warm. Optionally, you can serve them with whipped cream or vanilla ice cream.

Raspberry Hand Pies

Prep: **25** Min | Cook: **18** Min | Serves: **4 hand pies**

Ingredient:

For the pastry:
- 250g plain flour
- 125g unsalted butter, cold and cubed
- 2 tablespoons caster sugar
- 1/4 teaspoon salt
- 4-5 tablespoons cold water

For the filling:
- 200g fresh raspberries
- 50g caster sugar
- 1 tablespoon cornstarch
- 1/2 teaspoon lemon zest
- 1/2 teaspoon lemon juice

For assembly:
- 1 egg, beaten (for egg wash)
- Icing sugar, for dusting

Instruction:

1. In a mixing bowl, combine the plain flour, cold cubed unsalted butter, caster sugar, and salt. Use your fingertips to rub the butter into the flour mixture until it resembles breadcrumbs.
2. Gradually add the cold water, one tablespoon at a time, and mix until the dough comes together. Be careful not to overmix. Shape the dough into a ball, wrap it in plastic wrap, and refrigerate for 15 minutes.
3. In a separate bowl, gently toss the fresh raspberries with the caster sugar, cornstarch, lemon zest, and lemon juice until well coated. Divide the chilled dough into 4 equal portions and roll each portion out into a circle about 15cm in diameter.
4. In Zone 1, place one pastry circle in the air fryer basket.
5. Spoon a quarter of the raspberry filling onto one half of the pastry circle, leaving a border around the edges.
6. Fold the other half of the pastry circle over the filling to create a half-moon shape. Use a fork to seal the edges of the hand pie.
7. Brush the top of the hand pie with the beaten egg wash.
8. In Zone 1, place the hand pies. Select Zone 1, choose the BAKE program, and set the temperature to 180°C. Set the time to 15-18 minutes. Press the START/STOP button to begin cooking.
9. Let them cool for a few minutes. Dust the **hand pies** with icing sugar before serving.

Chapter 07: Desserts

Strawberry Shortcakes

Prep: **20** Min | Cook: **12** Min | Serves: **4 shortcakes**

Ingredient:

For the shortcakes:
- 250g self-raising flour
- 50g unsalted butter, cold and cubed
- 2 tablespoons caster sugar
- 150ml milk
- 1/2 teaspoon vanilla extract

For the strawberries:
- 500g fresh strawberries, hulled and sliced
- 2 tablespoons caster sugar

For the whipped cream:
- 300ml double cream
- 2 tablespoons icing sugar
- 1/2 teaspoon vanilla extract

Instruction:

1. In a mixing bowl, combine the self-raising flour and cold cubed unsalted butter. Use your fingertips to rub the butter into the flour until the mixture resembles breadcrumbs. Stir in the caster sugar.
2. In a separate jug, mix together the milk and vanilla extract. Gradually add the milk mixture to the dry ingredients, stirring until a soft dough forms.
3. Turn the dough out onto a lightly floured surface and knead it gently for a minute. Roll out the dough to a thickness of about 2cm.
4. Use a round cutter (approximately 7cm in diameter) to cut out 4 shortcakes from the dough.
5. In Zone 1, place the shortcakes. Select Zone 1, choose the BAKE program, and set the temperature to 180°C. Set the time to 10-12 minutes. Press the START/STOP button to begin cooking.
6. In a separate bowl, combine the sliced strawberries and caster sugar. Stir gently and let them macerate for 10 minutes.
7. In another bowl, whip the double cream, icing sugar, and vanilla extract until soft peaks form.
8. To assemble, slice each shortcake in half horizontally. Spoon some macerated strawberries onto the bottom half of each shortcake. Top with a dollop of whipped cream. Place the top half of the shortcake on top.
9. Optionally, you can dust the assembled **shortcakes** with a little icing sugar.

Apple Crisp

Prep: 20 Min | Cook: 25 Min | Serves: 4

Ingredient:

For the apple filling:
- 4 large apples, peeled, cored, and thinly sliced
- 50g caster sugar
- 1 tablespoon plain flour
- 1 teaspoon ground cinnamon
- 1/4 teaspoon ground nutmeg
- 1 tablespoon lemon juice

For the crisp topping:
- 100g plain flour
- 80g rolled oats
- 70g unsalted butter, cold and cubed
- 60g light brown sugar
- 1/4 teaspoon ground cinnamon
- 1/4 teaspoon salt

For serving:
- Vanilla ice cream or custard

Instruction:

1. In a mixing bowl, combine the sliced apples, caster sugar, plain flour, ground cinnamon, ground nutmeg, and lemon juice. Toss until the apples are well coated.
2. In Zone 1, place the apple mixture. Select Zone 1, choose the AIR FRY program, and set the temperature to 180°C. Set the time to 10 minutes. Press the START/STOP. After 10 minutes, remove the apple mixture from the air fryer and set it aside.
3. In a separate bowl, combine the plain flour, rolled oats, cold cubed unsalted butter, light brown sugar, ground cinnamon, and salt.
4. Use your fingertips to rub the butter into the dry ingredients until the mixture resembles coarse crumbs.
5. In Zone 2, spread the crisp topping evenly. Select Zone 2, choose the AIR FRY program, and set the temperature to 180°C. Set the time to 10-15 minutes. Press the START/STOP. Carefully remove the crisp topping from the air fryer and let it cool for a few minutes.
6. In individual serving dishes or a baking dish, layer the cooked apple mixture at the bottom. Sprinkle the crisp topping evenly over the apples. Return the dish(es) to Zone 2 of the air fryer.
7. Choose the BAKE program, and set the temperature to 180°C for 10-12 minutes. Press the START/STOP. Serve the **apple crisp** warm, with a scoop of vanilla ice cream or custard.

Chapter 07: Desserts

Jam Roly Poly

Prep: 15 Min | Cook: 30 Min | Serves: 4

Ingredient:

- 250g self-raising flour
- 125g suet
- 50g caster sugar
- 125ml milk
- Strawberry or raspberry jam
- Custard, to serve

Instruction:

1. In a mixing bowl, combine the self-raising flour, suet, and caster sugar.
2. Gradually add the milk to the dry ingredients, stirring until a soft dough forms.
3. Turn the dough out onto a lightly floured surface and roll it into a rectangle approximately 30cm x 20cm.
4. Spread a layer of strawberry or raspberry jam over the dough, leaving a small border around the edges.
5. Carefully roll up the dough from one of the longer sides, like a Swiss roll. Seal the edges by pressing them together.
6. In Zone 1, place the rolled dough in the air fryer basket.
7. Select Zone 1, choose the BAKE program, and set the temperature to 180°C. Set the time to 25-30 minutes.
8. Press the START/STOP button to begin cooking.
9. After 25-30 minutes of air frying in Zone 1, the Jam Roly Poly should be golden brown and cooked through.
10. Carefully remove the Jam Roly Poly from the air fryer and let it cool for a few minutes.
11. Slice the Jam **Roly Poly** into portions and serve warm with custard.

Eton Mess Balls

Prep: **10** Min | Cook: **10** Min | Serves: **4**

Ingredient:

- 125 g strawberries, hulled and quartered
- 125 g raspberries
- 200 ml double cream
- 1 teaspoon vanilla extract
- 250 g meringue nests, crushed
- 1 tablespoon icing sugar

Instruction:

1. In a large bowl, combine the strawberries, raspberries, double cream, and vanilla extract. Stir gently until combined.
2. Add the crushed meringue nests and icing sugar to the bowl. Fold gently until the ingredients are well combined.
3. Using a tablespoon, scoop the mixture into balls and place them on a baking tray lined with parchment paper.
4. Place the baking tray in Zone 1 of the Ninja Dual Zone Air Fryer. Select Zone 1 and select the AIR FRY program. Set the temperature to 180°C and the time to 10 minutes. Press the START/STOP button to begin cooking.
5. After 10 minutes, check the Eton Mess balls. They should be golden brown and crispy on the outside, and soft and gooey on the inside.
6. Carefully remove the Eton Mess balls from the air fryer and let them cool for a few minutes before serving.
7. Sprinkle some chopped nuts, such as almonds or pistachios, on top of the balls for added texture and flavor.
8. Serve the **Eton Mess Balls** alongside a fresh green salad or roasted vegetables to add a refreshing touch to the plate.

Chapter 07: Desserts

Flapjacks

Prep: **10** Min | Cook: **25** Min | Serves: **12**

Ingredient:

- 200g unsalted butter
- 200g golden syrup
- 200g light brown sugar
- 400g porridge oats

Instruction:

1. In a saucepan, melt the unsalted butter, golden syrup, and light brown sugar over low heat, stirring until well combined.
2. In Zone 1, place the porridge oats in the air fryer basket.
3. Select Zone 1, choose the AIR FRY program, and set the temperature to 160°C. Set the time to 5 minutes.
4. Press the START/STOP button to begin air frying the oats. This step helps to toast the oats slightly and enhance their flavor.
5. After 5 minutes, carefully remove the toasted oats from the air fryer and set them aside.
6. In a large mixing bowl, combine the melted butter mixture with the toasted oats. Stir until all the oats are well coated.
7. In Zone 1, spread the oat mixture evenly in the air fryer basket.
8. Select Zone 1, choose the AIR FRY program, and set the temperature to 160°C. Set the time to 15-20 minutes.
9. Press the START/STOP button to begin cooking.
10. After 15-20 minutes, the flapjacks should be golden brown and set.
11. Carefully remove the flapjacks from the air fryer and let them cool in the basket for a few minutes.
12. Transfer the flapjacks to a cutting board and slice them into bars or squares while they are still warm.
13. Allow the **flapjacks** to cool completely before serving.

Bread and Butter Pudding

Prep: **15** Min | Cook: **20** Min | Serves: **4**

Ingredient:

- 8 slices of day-old bread
- 50g unsalted butter, softened
- 50g raisins or sultanas
- 2 tbsp demerara sugar
- 2 large eggs
- 300ml whole milk
- 50g caster sugar
- 1 tsp vanilla extract
- Ground nutmeg for sprinkling

Instruction:

1. Spread butter on one side of each bread slice. Cut the bread slices diagonally to form triangles.
2. Arrange half of the bread triangles, buttered side up, in Zone 1 of the Ninja Dual Zone Air Fryer.
3. Sprinkle half of the raisins or sultanas and demerara sugar over the bread. Layer the remaining bread triangles on top, again with the buttered side up.
4. Sprinkle the remaining raisins or sultanas and demerara sugar over the bread.
5. In a bowl, whisk together the eggs, milk, caster sugar, and vanilla extract. Pour the egg mixture evenly over the bread layers in the air fryer. Sprinkle ground nutmeg on top.
6. Select Zone 1, choose the BAKE program, and set the temperature to 180°C. Set the time to 20 minutes.
7. Press the START/STOP button to begin cooking.
8. After 10 minutes of cooking, carefully open the air fryer and flip the tbread. Continue cooking for the remaining 10 minutes or until the bread and butter pudding is golden brown and set.
9. Once cooked, remove the Bread and Butter Pudding from the air fryer and let it cool slightly. Serve the **Bread and Butter Pudding** warm as a delightful British dessert.

Chapter 07: Desserts

Banoffee Pie Bites

Prep: **15** Min | Cook: **10** Min | Serves: **4**

Ingredient:

- 8 digestive biscuits
- 50g unsalted butter, melted
- 1 ripe banana
- 200g dulce de leche or caramel sauce
- 200ml double cream
- 1 tbsp icing sugar
- Grated chocolate or cocoa powder for garnish

Instruction:

1. Crush the digestive biscuits into fine crumbs using a food processor or by placing them in a sealed bag and crushing with a rolling pin.
2. In a bowl, mix the biscuit crumbs with melted butter until well combined.
3. Press the biscuit mixture into the bottom of Zone 1 of the Ninja Dual Zone Air Fryer to form a crust layer.
4. Select Zone 1, choose the AIR FRY program, and set the temperature to 180°C. Set the time to 5 minutes.
5. Press the START/STOP button to begin cooking. After 5 minutes, carefully remove the biscuit base from the air fryer and let it cool.
6. Once the biscuit base has cooled, slice the banana into thin rounds.
7. Spread a layer of dulce de leche or caramel sauce over the biscuit base. Arrange the banana slices on top of the caramel layer.
8. In a bowl, whip the double cream and icing sugar together until soft peaks form.
9. Spoon or pipe the whipped cream over the banana layer. Sprinkle grated chocolate or dust with cocoa powder for garnish.
10. Place the Banoffee Pie Bites in Zone 1 of the air fryer.
11. Select Zone 1, choose the BAKE program, and set the temperature to 180°C for 5 minutes. Press the START/STOP.
12. After 5 minutes, carefully remove the Banoffee Pie Bites from the air fryer. Let them cool slightly before serving. Serve the **Banoffee Pie Bites** as a scrumptious British dessert.

Printed in Great Britain
by Amazon